W9-DIO-098

MACKINAC ISLAND
ITS HISTORY IN PICTURES

by Eugene T. Petersen

Mackinac State Historic Parks, Mackinac Island, Michigan

©1973 Mackinac State Historic Parks

Design - Eddy Graphic Design, Kalamazoo, Michigan

1st Printing	4,000 copies
2nd Printing	3,000 copies
3rd Printing	3,000 copies
4th Printing	2,500 copies
5th Printing	2,500 copies
6th Printing	2,500 copies
7th Printing	5,000 copies
8th Printing	4,000 copies

TABLE OF CONTENTS

FOREWORD

Since Mackinac Island was founded in 1780 during the American Revolution, we are publishing this book as part of the Mackinac Island State Park Commission's official Bicentennial Program.

The military and the fur trade dominated the Island's life during the 19th century, but tourists have been visiting its historic and scenic attractions for more than 125 years. Mackinac Island is one of the most popular tourist resorts in the Midwest. Each summer over half a million people make their pilgrimage to the "Island of the Big Turtle."

Visitors to Mackinac have described the Island with pen, brush, and camera. Untold numbers of pictures of Mackinac Island survive and are dispersed throughout the country. During the past several years the Mackinac Island State Park Commission has collected originals and copies of several thousand Island pictures as an aid to the restoration of the historic buildings at Fort Mackinac and elsewhere. These pictures, especially the photographs which so faithfully record a split second of the past, have proven invaluable in making accurate restoration possible.

Rather than keep these rich resources to ourselves, we have decided to make a sampling available to all. This selection covers the broad range of Mackinac's varied history from the fur trade to the tourists. A careful examination of the pictures will show how much of the past still remains and yet how much has been lost.

Mackinac has thus far resisted the pressures of our automobile-dominated society. Transportation by leisurely horse-drawn vehicle prevails, and one can recapture a deep feeling and understanding of the past.

For those who have visited Mackinac Island it is hoped that this book will evoke a multitude of fond memories. For those whose path has never led to the area, this publication will serve as a record of a vanishing heritage and a dream to visit in the future.

Thus we add *Mackinac Island, Its History in Pictures* to the Mackinac Island State Park Commission's growing list of publications about the Straits of Mackinac. We are certain that it will find as honored a place on your shelves as Mackinac has found in your hearts.

Mackinac Island State Park Commission

INTRODUCTION

A photograph, someone once said, "is a kind of miracle."
It is a moment of history frozen for all time. Unlike the words that flow from the typewriter of an historian, whose effectiveness depends on his perception, scholarship, and ability to communicate, a picture instantly shows it "as it was" and makes every viewer an authority on that split second of history.

A series of photographs arranged chronologically can tell us not only how it was, but more significantly how it has changed. These pictures, which include drawings as well as later photographs, are in themselves a chronicle of Mackinac Island history since 1780. We can see the crude dwellings and warehouses of the early French and British employees of the American Fur Company, whose buildings along Market Street have fortunately survived to this day. The role of the military on Mackinac Island is visually traced through the evolution of Fort Mackinac buildings, as well as the old Indian dormitory. Patrick Sinclair's 1780 British fort on that high bluff above the harbor is somewhat different from the military reservation turned over to the State of Michigan in 1895, but the fact that even one of these American Revolutionary era structures remains is amazing.

In the chronicle of change we are reminded that the way people earned their living and spent their leisure time determined the physical appearance of their community. By the mid-1850's the fur economy had given way to the fish economy, and the shops and houses along main street were characteristic of the fishermen, the fish processors, the coopers and the boat builders. When the fish ran out, the people turned to serving the tourists, and the hotels, restaurants and gift shops brought yet another appearance to the Island. Some of the visitors stayed and built their large Victorian homes on the bluffs. If they did not earn their money on Mackinac Island, they spent some of it here and so contributed to the tourist-oriented economy which is now the means of livelihood for most of the permanent residents.

In some respects we are all antiquarians and, as such, are suspicious of change. We look fondly back at the "good old days" and wish that it could be so again. But change is not all bad, even on such an historic island as Mackinac. Today it is difficult for most of us to think of Mackinac Island without the Grand Hotel and the summer houses on the bluffs. Yet in 1846 the eminent poet, William Cullen Bryant, as we have seen in the frontispiece, predicted the construction of boarding houses and summer cottages with a "kind of regret."

These pictures also let us second-guess our predecessors who wittingly or unwittingly destroyed an interesting building either by design or neglect. It would indeed have been nice if some of these structures had been preserved as examples of 19th century architecture. But let us also give credit for what has been preserved: The buildings downtown and at Fort Mackinac that are now museums, and especially the large number of privately-owned Victorian homes and business places whose owners have managed to adapt them to modern use despite staggering maintenance costs. These owners are often the unsung heroes, but their dedication to the preservation of the Mackinac scene deserves the accolades of those of us who love this tremendously interesting island.

The choice of pictures to be included in an album such as this is difficult. With literally hundreds of scenes available, some have to be left out. I have tried to develop a running chronology of the Island's history and, therefore, have chosen drawings and photographs that contribute to that development. In many cases I have had to leave out technically excellent photographs because they added nothing to the narrative. Conversely, I have chosen some pictures that are of marginal quality and some that are downright poor in order to show an important facet of Mackinac Island's history.

Speaking of quality, you will notice vast differences in the photographs. In many cases the reproduction you see in the album is third or fourth generation, in other words, a copy of a copy, and in each copy some sharpness is lost. Also, I have made enlargements of details in some photographs to emphasize a point. This again lessens the quality.

Dating pictures and drawings is very difficult. Unfortunately, most photographers are not historians. They seldom bother to record the time a picture was taken or to identify its subjects. Consequently, I have had to make educated guesses based on known dates, for example, when the tower was put up at Fenton's Bazaar or when the Iroquois Hotel was built. Rather than repeatedly saying "about --," I have in most cases assigned the closest year I can, recognizing full well it could be somewhat inaccurate. Whenever possible, I have identified persons in the pictures.

Except where otherwise noted, the pictures are from the collections of the Mackinac Island State Park Commission. Many were obtained in the course of research for restoration of Fort Mackinac. Some have been reproduced from 18th century travel accounts, steamboat and railroad promotional brochures, and from various editions of Dwight Kelton's *Annals of Fort Mackinac*, John R. Bailey's *Mackinac, formerly Michilimackinac*, J. A. Van Fleet's *Old and New Mackinac*, Meade C. Williams' *Early Mackinac*, and E. O. Wood's *Historic Mackinac*. These useful volumes are long out of print. The largest single source of pictures was William Gardiner's collection of glass negatives numbering over 3,500.

Many individuals, libraries, and archives have been helpful and generous in making available their Mackinac pictures. I would like to thank Katherine Bond, Mr. and Mrs. Robert Doud, Mr. and Mrs. Robert Benjamin and Mr. and Mrs. Robert Bailey of Mackinac Island. The Mackinac Island Historical Society allowed me to copy its collection donated by the late Edward Cudahy. Other pictures are reproduced through the courtesy of the Grand Hotel, McCord Museum of McGill University, Clarke Historical Library of Central Michigan University, Burton Historical Collection of the Detroit Public Library, Chicago Historical Society, Michigan History Division and the William L. Clements Library and Michigan Historical Collections of the University of Michigan. A number of rare photographs collected by the late Alicia Poole and donated by Mrs. Dana Seeley have also been used. Special thanks must go to Mrs. Maria Douma of Petoskey, who donated the entire glass slide collection of 19th century Island photographer William H. Gardiner. When the thousands of portraits in this collection are identified, it will be a fairly complete "who's who" of Mackinac Island's cottagers for the years 1880 to 1920.

IDENTIFICATION MAP

1. British Landing
2. Battlefield
3. Fort Holmes
4. Sugar Loaf
5. Fort Mackinac
6. West Bluff
7. Annex
8. Harrisonville
9. Grand Hotel
10. Biddle Point
11. Old Government Pasture-Golf Course
12. Market Street
13. Main Street
14. Docks
15. Fort Gardens — Marquette Park
16. East Bluff
17. Island House
18. Ste. Ann's Church
19. Mission Church
20. Mission House
21. Mission Point
22. Arch Rock

Mackinac Island is the most impressive land area in the Straits of Mackinac. Contrasting with severely flat landscapes on the mainland, its high limestone bluffs stand out in sharp relief from every direction. Its eight mile circumference is broken by a small crescent shaped harbor on the south side which offered not only deep water close to shore, but good protection from the prevailing westerly winds.

SOLDIERS, FUR AND FISH

The geography of Mackinac Island has been important in its history. The geological limestone formations we know as Sugar Loaf, Arch Rock, and Skull Cave, as well as the distinctive high bluffs, have attracted interest for a long time. Prehistoric Indians camped along the shores and buried their dead in the caves. Father Claude Allouez, who first described the Island in 1669, was particularly impressed with the 150-foot bluffs in the otherwise flat area. In 1780, when the British commander Patrick Sinclair looked for a place to move his mainland fort, he chose Mackinac Island because these same bluffs gave him security from enemy forces.

For the next fifty years, under British and American rule, the Island prospered as the midwest fur processing center. Eastern capital created the Market Street buildings of the Astor Fur Company and the private homes of the managers who worked for the company. In the 1820's the religious missionary zeal of some Boston Presbyterians introduced to the Island an eastern church architecture that could hardly be distinguished from its New England models.

In the 1840's the economy of the Island took a new turn. The fur was gone, and so was John Jacob Astor's company. The native English, French and Indians were joined by waves of new immigrants, such as the Irish, who came to America to escape the potato famine and to find their fortunes. They brought with them skills in carpentry and a determination to make good. With scarcely a break, the fur economy became the fish economy, and Mackinac Island became the center for processing of Great Lakes whitefish and lake trout.

Fish processing brought new construction. New docks were built and older ones enlarged. Warehouses for salting and icing the fish appeared on the docks and along main street. The coopers' shops, where the shipping barrels were fabricated, were scattered throughout the town. Distinctive Mackinac boats were adapted for Mackinac's fishermen who braved all kinds of weather to set out miles of gill nets daily.

Most of the buildings were not impressive by later standards. Bark-covered sheds, lean-to's and rather dilapidated, unpainted residences predominated. Many Island homes were separated by picket fences in various states of repair, but fences were necessary to keep the cattle at home and out of the neighbor's garden. Hard work, long hours and low income for most people left little opportunity to improve their own property.

Above the town changes were also taking place at Fort Mackinac. The small British fort that the Americans won by treaty after the Revolution and again after the War of 1812 was enlarged to house and supply increasing numbers of United States soldiers. When there was no longer room within the stockade walls, the Major's and Captain's quarters, as well as the bakery and surgeon's house, were built outside. The blacksmith shop, vegetable and animal barns appeared below the bluff near the soldiers' garden. As the century wore on the threat from British Canada and the Indians were no longer real, and Fort Mackinac's usefulness was limited to that of a training post.

Near the end of the century a new economy based on tourism was to bring many more physical changes to Mackinac Island.

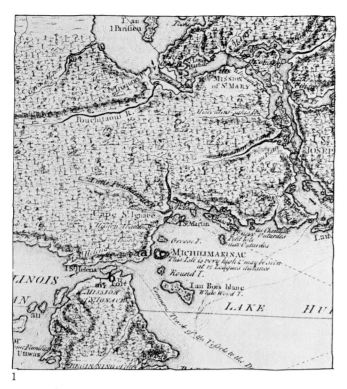

1

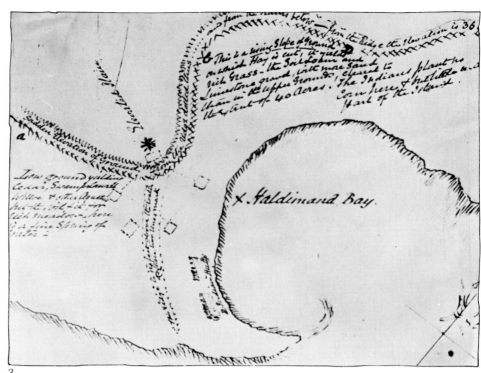

3

2

1. For over three centuries the Straits of Mackinac have been occupied by military establishments. In 1671 Father Jacques Marquette established his mission on the north side of the Straits and was protected by a detachment of French soldiers at Fort De Buade (a). Sieur de la mothe Cadillac abandoned the post in the late 1690's and shortly after erected a new fortification at Detroit, but in 1715 the French returned and built a strong, palisaded fort on the southern mainland (b). The British took over Fort Michilimackinac in 1761 and, twenty years later, reestablished it in the center of the Straits on the Island (c) which, as this 1761 English map indicates, was "very high and may be seen at 12 leagues distance."

2. The mainland Fort Michilimackinac, which the British took from the French in 1761, was poorly placed. Although built close to the water, which made it easy to provision, the flat ground around the fort made it difficult to see landward. The shifting beach sand piled in mounds near the blockhouses to afford excellent enemy cover. Moreover, the wooden structures, many of which dated from the 1740's, required constant maintenance. When the American Revolutionary War spread westward in the late 1770's, Lt. Governor Patrick Sinclair, the commandant, looked to Mackinac Island as a new fort site. The mainland fort shown here is a recent reconstruction.

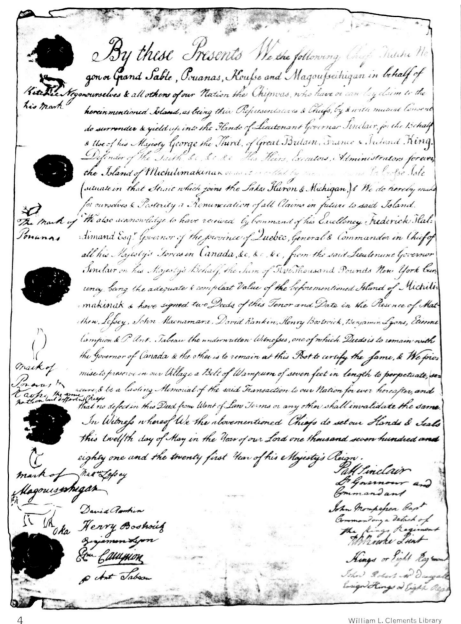

William L. Clements Library

4

5

Chicago Historical Society

6

History Division, Michigan Department of State

3. In the fall of 1779 Sinclair spent three days "from sun to sun" examining Mackinac Island. He found great numbers of beech, maple and cedar trees, as well as limestone outcroppings which could be used for building construction. The soil was suitable for growing vegetables, and there were convenient springs. Most important, however, the high bluffs offered a strategic military position in pleasant contrast with the low, flat and sandy location of the mainland fort. He enclosed this sketch of the harbor and high ground in a letter to his superiors.

4. When permission came to move the fort to the Island, there remained only the formality of purchasing it from the local Chippewa Indians. This was readily arranged. For £5,000, New York currency, "being the adequate and compleat value of the before mentioned Island of Michilimackinac," four local chiefs signed this deed, and ownership was transferred to His Majesty.

5. Sinclair put his fort high on the bluff overlooking the harbor. As every military engineer knows, it is strategically desirable to command high ground, and from this vantage point he could observe all traffic through the Straits of Mackinac. Below his guns on either side of the fort's approach, the private houses and barns of the French and British fur traders soon sprung up. It was, as a later Fort Mackinac commander put it, "an island fortress built by nature for herself." This sketch was made by a British officer, Col. Henry F. Ainslie, in 1842 after the Americans were in possession.

6. No known portrait of Governor Sinclair exists, but this silhouette was made much later in life, after he returned to England.

1. Following the American Revolution and the Treaty of Ghent, the boundary lines between the new democracy and British Canada were drawn to include Fort Mackinac on the American side. A United States force occupied the Straits post in 1796. There was no artist present to sketch the turnover, but one of the American soldiers lost this jacket button on the garrison parade ground. The British moved across the international boundary to St. Joseph Island about forty miles away.

2. The War of 1812 was a series of frustrations for the Americans at Mackinac. The British on St. Joseph Island were the first to learn of the outbreak of hostilities and, under cover of darkness, landed an expeditionary force on the north end of the Island on July 17, 1812. The following morning the American commander of Fort Mackinac, Lt. Porter Hanks, learned that the United States and England were at war at the same time he discovered a large force of the enemy and their Indian allies encamped on the high ground behind his fort. He surrendered. Two years later, an American naval force sailed into the harbor prepared to blast Fort Mackinac off the bluff, only to find their ships' guns could not be raised enough to hit the buildings. Major George Croghan then disembarked his soldiers at the north end of the Island. But the British, who after all had invented the idea, were ready and repulsed the invaders after a stiff battle. You can still stand at "British Landing" like these 1885 American tourists and contemplate what went wrong.

3. The 1814 battle was fought a half mile from British Landing on Dousman's farm. The Americans appeared at the edge of the woods, led by their second in command, Major Andrew Holmes. As they advanced, a small group of Indians who were protecting the British left flank opened fire. The British fired their artillery from the high ground, and the Americans hastily withdrew. When the smoke cleared, the Americans counted sixty-four casualties, including Holmes.

4. Major Andrew Hunter Holmes, a promising young American officer who died in the attempt to recapture Fort Mackinac in 1814, was buried in Detroit. When in 1834 his body was exhumed, the casket was said to contain six heavy cannon balls placed there to sink the body, had the British attempted to capture the vessel which carried it from Mackinac Island.

5. United States Engineers drew this map of the Island after 1815. Fort George, which the British constructed in 1812 on the high ground behind Fort Mackinac, was later renamed Fort Holmes in honor of the American officer who was killed in battle.

1

2

3

Library of Congress

National Archives

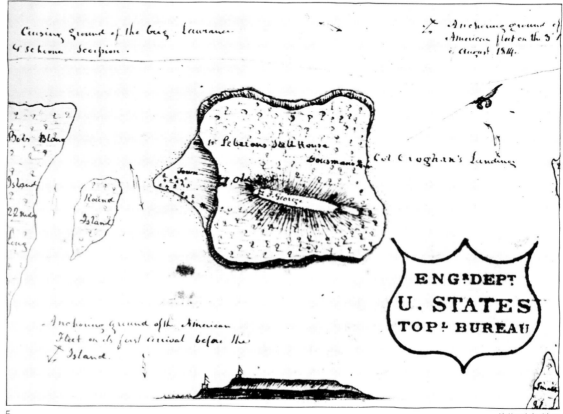

5

National Archives

1

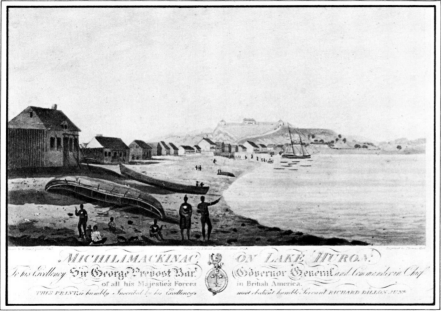

2

3

McCord Museum, McGill University

16

4

5

Burton Historical Collection

6

Peabody Museum, Harvard University

1. A pro-British Mackinac Islander who cooperated with the invaders in 1812 was Dr. David Mitchell. As an English army surgeon, he welcomed the English occupation, a fact that made him *persona non grata* with the Americans when they reoccupied the fort after the war. His home, one of the Island's most impressive, still stood in the 1890's when this photograph was taken. Mitchell left with the British army and never returned although his wife continued to reside in the house. One contemporary described her as of French and Sioux Indian extraction, extremely pretty, with "soft and gentle manners." A post doctor at Fort Crawford is supposed to have committed suicide "over an unsuccessful attachment he had for her." Apparently she did not lack for company during her days on Mackinac Island.

2. One of the earliest sketches of the Island was done by Richard Dillon of Montreal in 1813. The picketed fort with its two blockhouses dominates the bluff. In the harbor a two-masted schooner lies close to shore while supplies are being unloaded from smaller craft nearby. In the foreground some Indians are lolling on the beach near their immense birch bark canoes. One of them is smoking his pipe. French and British fur trader homes are strung along the shore.

3. Particularly interesting are the traders' houses. In this detail from Dillon's sketch we see a rather square, one-story structure with a small gable. It is log construction, possibly weather-boarded. The very high picket fence around the building was for protection from the Indians. The poles which seem to prop up the front of the building indicate this home was already quite old in 1812.

4. In this detail the large two-story warehouses for storage of furs are in evidence. The economic life of the Island was the fur trade, just as it had been at Michilimackinac on the mainland since 1715.

5. This 1820 sketch is drawn from a different vantage point, but it shows the cluster of houses along the waterfront to the left of the fort. Also, directly below are several large military buildings surrounded by a fence. The long picket-lined ramp leading diagonally up to Fort Mackinac's south sally port was an Island landmark that remains to this day. In the center foreground the oft-sketched Indian sits quietly smoking his peace pipe.

6. This unique picture of two Ottawa chiefs from Michilimackinac was painted about 1814 by Sir Josiah Jebb, when these Indians went to Canada to hold a Council with the British officials. Notice the top hat carried by the one and the large silver brooches worn by both. Also of interest is the large birch bark canoe in the background. This is the earliest picture we have of Indians from Michilimackinac.

1. After the War of 1812 and the Americans' return, thanks to the peace treaty, the fur trade reached its zenith. One important effect of the war was that by Congressional action only American citizens could trade with the Indians within the United States. As a result, John Jacob Astor of New York bought out the English traders of the Southwest Company and formed one of the largest business enterprises of its day, the American Fur Company, with headquarters on Mackinac Island. The company's buildings are shown in this 1870 photograph: (a). The Company Storehouse. (b). Robert Stuart House. (c). Clerks' Quarters.

2. The Clerks' Quarters housed the men who processed the furs in Astor's warehouse and also his agents who lived and traded with the Indians at their hunting grounds during the winter months. With time and money on their hands, they enlivened the Island's summer social scene.

3. By the time this photograph was taken in 1903, the warehouse and Stuart house were joined by a long porch and converted to a hotel. The warehouse was used to store the Company's goods for the Indian trade and also to process the furs. Each fall the Company sent its agents to bargain for furs, and each spring, when the ice broke, they returned with their huge canoes loaded with tons of furs. On the left is Mackinac County's court house before 1882. The most important case tried there was People v. Pond, which involved a fatal shooting. Augustus Pond shot and killed a man who was destroying some of his outbuildings. Found guilty in this court, Pond appealed to the Michigan Supreme Court, which in a landmark decision reversed the lower court and set Pond free on the grounds that he had the right to protect himself, his family, and his property because, "A man's house is his castle."

4. Robert Stuart was Astor's representative on Mackinac Island. His house on Market Street was the social center for the Islanders and for many of Mackinac's visitors during the 1820's and 1830's. One Easterner who sampled the Stuarts' hospitality remarked that the evening "would have done credit to New York or Philadelphia." After Stuart died in Chicago in 1848, the vessel carrying his body to Detroit for burial stopped at Mackinac so that his Island friends could pay their last respects.

5. One of the pieces of American Fur Company furniture now on exhibit in the Stuart House museum is a desk where some Company scribe carefully kept his ledger.

6. This 1856 photograph of Market Street looking east is the oldest view of this important Island thoroughfare. Most of the small homes still have cedar bark roofs. An exception is the pillored residence on the left which was the home of Constance Saltonstall Patton, whose husband was prominent in the fur trade.

7. One who worked with Stuart in the fur business was Edward Biddle, a member of the distinguished Philadelphia Biddle family. His home, one of the oldest on the Island, is the first building on the left.

8. The Biddle house was not exactly a candidate for *Better Homes and Gardens* when this picture was taken a hundred years after its owner died. However, its survival makes it possible for us to see a good example of early architecture on Mackinac Island.

1

2

Library of Congress

4

Mackinac Island Historical Society

5

6

8

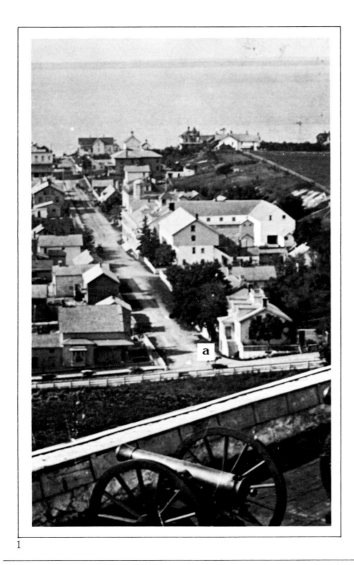

1

2

1. On the east end of Market Street stood the American Fur Company retail store (a). Although the building had undergone changes when this photograph was made in 1885, it remained one of the most significant sites on Mackinac Island. In 1822 a group of the Company's agents and *engagees* were doing their shopping (and probably clowning in the process) when one of them, Alexis St. Martin, was accidentally shot in the abdomen. Gurdon Hubbard, who witnessed the event, said it was a shotgun blast two to three feet away. Fort Mackinac's Dr. William Beaumont managed to save the young man's life. However, the stomach wound never healed properly, and the Doctor was able to observe and later to experiment with the heretofore unknown process of digestion. In one of the earliest welfare cases on the Island, borough records show that Dr. Beaumont was paid fifty dollars from December, 1822 to June, 1823 "for surgical and medicine for Alexis St. Martin, a pauper."

2. If Mrs. Mitchell of the "soft and gentle manners" is remembered, so also should be Madame La Framboise. Mrs. Juliette Kinzie, who visited the Island in 1830, described her as a tall and commanding figure whose husband had taught her to read and write. After his murder by a Winnebago Indian, she took over his business. She visited the trading posts and supervised the buying and selling of furs. She

also found time to teach a group of pupils daily in basic education as well as religion. All of this is more remarkable considering that Madame La Framboise was a full-blooded Ottawa Indian. This was her home. After her death, she was buried under the altar of Ste. Ann's Church. Her daughter, Josette, married Captain John Pierce of Fort Mackinac, who was the brother of President Franklin Pierce.

3. The breakup of the ice in the spring was the signal for the population of Mackinac Island to swell from about 500 permanent residents to over 3,000. Not only the American Fur Company *engagees* who had spent the winter months negotiating with the Indians for their furs, but the Indians themselves descended on the place. Mrs. Kinzie, who stood on the shore in 1830, said it was not unusual to see one hundred canoes accompanied by the large fur-burdened Mackinac boats approach from the west. This sketch was made by an unknown artist in the 1840's.

4. The Mackinac boat, which was distinctive of the Great Lakes, had two masts and a jib. Pointed at bow and stern, with graceful lines, it was very seaworthy and admirably suited to the inland waters.

5. Mackinac boats were still widely used as late as 1890, when this photograph was made in the harbor.

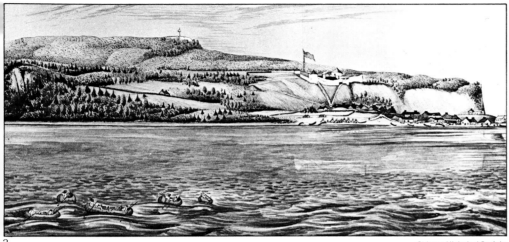

3

Chicago Historical Society

4

5

1. In 1819, the first steamboat on the Great Lakes, *Walk-in-the-Water*, stopped at Mackinac Island on her maiden voyage. No doubt, the entire Island population was at the dock to see the phenomenon of a boat that moved without oars or sail. The significance of the excursion was not lost on contemporaries, as indicated by the *Mercantile Advertizer,* which stated unabashedly that the trip so resembled "the legendary expeditions in the heroic ages of Greece" that many distinguished citizens "engaged passage for this splendid adventure." Among the arrivals, incidentally, was Dr. William Beaumont. *Walk-in-the-Water* went down in Lake Erie shortly after her Mackinac visit, but she inaugurated the era of steamboating on the Great Lakes.

2. Shortly after the War of 1812 the village embarked upon self government. Governor William Woodbridge of the Michigan Territory established the borough of Mackinac in 1817, and soon after its residents elected three trustees and William H. Puthuff, president. About this time some unknown artist made this map, which clearly shows not only the original line of buildings along Haldimand Bay, but clusters of new houses between Market and Main Streets. Likely it was the growing congestion of wooden buildings that moved the city fathers to adopt a strong fire protection ordinance as one of their first actions. It provided that all chimneys be "swept" every two weeks and all stovepipes have metal shields where they went through wooden roofs. Moreover, the law provided that at the first cry of fire "every housekeeper shall turn out every male capable of assisting" or pay a ten dollar fine.

3. This 1842 sketch, which appeared in Castelnau's "Vues . . . de Amerique du Nord," is one of the earliest done from the bluff at this location. The artist shows the fort on the left and the town pasture at the right. Most interesting is the busy harbor scene, which includes an early steamboat. Generally visitors were welcome at this remote northern island, but one exception was during 1832 when, by local ordinance, no vessel was allowed to dock under penalty of a hundred dollar fine until it had been inspected by the borough warden and found free of *Cholera Morbus.*

4. When C. F. Davis sat on the shore of Round Island in 1839, he sketched the fort and the borough houses, but he also drew three important structures to the right of Fort Mackinac that represented the relationships of the Federal government and a private missionary group with the Indians. The Indian Dormitory (a) was built in 1838; the Indian Agency House (b) dates from shortly after the War of 1812; and the Mission Church and school buildings (c) were built in 1825-1829.

5. The Agency House was the home and office of the United States Indian agent in the Michigan Territory. It was his job to deal with all problems relating to the Indians and to allot yearly annuities in conformity with the terms of the various Indian treaties. He also had to win their support from the British, a difficult task because the local Chippewa and Ottawa, who were definitely pro-English, saw nothing wrong with picking up the American allotment and then moving on to Fort Malden to see what the British had to offer. And the English, who still had visions of regaining Mackinac, were not niggardly in their gifts.

1

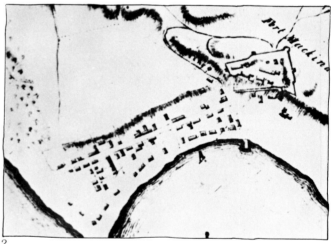

2

4

3

Burton Historical Collection

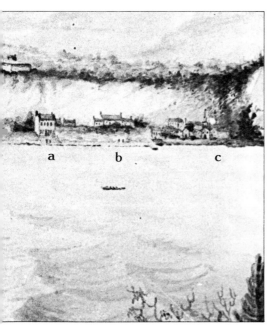

a   b   c

5

ALGIC RESEARCHES,

COMPRISING

INQUIRIES RESPECTING THE MENTAL
CHARACTERISTICS

OF THE

NORTH AMERICAN INDIANS

FIRST SERIES

INDIAN TALES AND LEGENDS

IN TWO VOLUMES
VOL. I

BY HENRY ROWE SCHOOLCRAFT

Author of a Narrative Journal of Travels to the Source of the Mississippi;
Travels in the Central Portions of the Mississippi Valley;
An Expedition to Itasca Lake, &c.

NEW-YORK:

HARPER & BROTHERS, 82 CLIFF-STREET

1839.

1

2

Chicago Historical Society

1. Henry R. Schoolcraft, who served from 1833 to 1841, was the most able of the Indian agents. Schoolcraft not only dealt fairly with the Indians (his wife was a full-blooded Chippewa) but took the opportunity to observe the Indian first hand. He published over thirty books, including a study of their legends and customs in 1839 entitled *Algic Researches*.

2. When the Indians came to Mackinac, they brought their teepees and their families with them, as this 1842 sketch shows. Many accounts written in the 1830's tell of as many as three thousand camped along the shore. Mrs. Kinzie said their "presents" included blankets, broadcloth, calico, guns, kettles, traps, silver armbands, bracelets, earbobs, looking glasses, combs and trinkets. They could also obtain liquor most times, and drunkenness was a problem for the authorities. The village records of 1856 show that two more night watchmen were to be employed "during the coming Indian payment."

3. Perhaps to alleviate the crowded conditions along the beach, Schoolcraft wrote an interesting provision into the Treaty of Washington in 1836. In return for ceding the northern half of Michigan and in addition to the usual monetary allotments, the United States agreed to build a "dormitory for Indians visiting Mackinac Island." Presumably this meant the chiefs only, as the building which opened in 1838 could hardly accommodate more than a handful of the summer visitors. This humanitarian gesture was never successful, and after 1848 the building, shown here on the right, was used for various non-Indian purposes. From 1870 to 1960 it was the Island school.

4. This front view was drawn in 1874 and shows a fence separating the school from the soldiers' garden. The building at the top of the bluff is the post surgeon's quarters.

5. Christian missionary activity among the Indians has always been strong. The first white man to winter on Mackinac Island was Father Claude Dablon, a Jesuit priest, who built a bark chapel in 1670. The following year Father Jacques Marquette established the first permanent mission at St. Ignace. When Governor Sinclair moved the fort in 1780, he went to great pains to move the Catholic church building from Michilimackinac across the ice to Mackinac Island. It was not until the 1820's, however, that the Protestants established a base here. At the southeast end of the Island they built Mission Church (a) and Mission House (b).

6. In June, 1820 the Reverend Jedediah Morse (father of Samuel B. Morse, inventor of the telegraph) preached one of the first Protestant sermons on Mackinac Island. Three years later, the Reverend William Ferry, sponsored by the United Foreign Mission Society of New York, was sent to establish a school for Indian children. Under Rev. and and Mrs. Ferry's able direction, the school prospered. Children were housed in the Mission and taught a practical curriculum that included trade skills and gardening for the boys and domestic arts for the girls. In the early 1830's enrollment reached a peak of two hundred. However, by 1837 lack of support led to its closing and the end of an experiment in Christian and practical education. The school shown here was built in 1825.

4

6

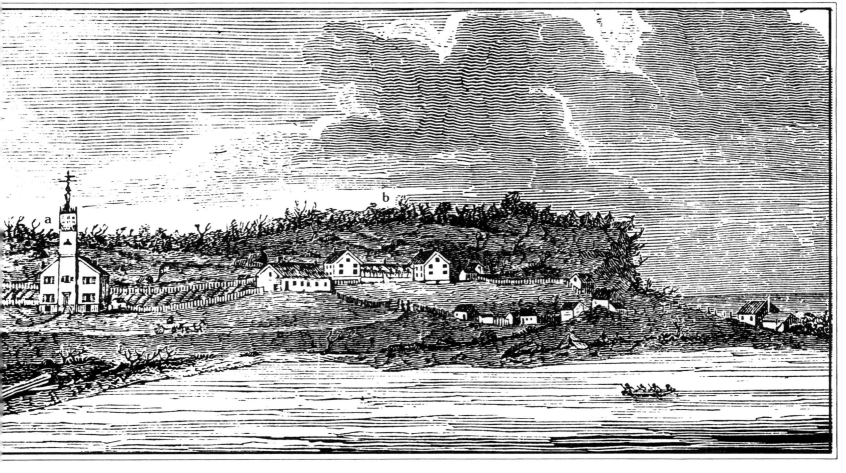

1

Library of Congress

2

Rev. Wm. Ferry

Mrs. Ferry

1. Mission Church, where Rev. Ferry preached to the Indians and the local Protestants, dates from 1829. After Ferry left the Island, Protestant services were held at irregular intervals throughout the years. The Reverend J. A. Van Fleet, who preached intermittently during the 1860's, said there were only fifty adult Protestants and complained that one Sunday school teacher spent his evenings in saloons in company with gamblers and drinkers and thought nothing of drinking "all Wednesday night and attending prayer meeting Thursday." This, to Rev. Van Fleet, was "burying the Lord and the Devil entirely too near together." A few years earlier the village trustees had declared the graveyard at Mission Church a public nuisance. Anyone caught bringing bodies there for burial was subject to a fifty dollar fine "for each offense."

2. With its high pulpit and separate pews, the interior is similar in character to eastern churches which were familiar to Rev. Ferry.

3. By 1834 the fur business was dead. Astor sold out his Mackinac holdings and moved his base of operation to the west coast. For nearly two hundred years the beaver had been the only business at the Straits of Mackinac, but now its people had to turn to other ways to make their fortunes. Fortunately there was another natural resource at their doorsteps, and from 1840 to 1880 the fishery business dominated their lives.

This 1875 photograph of downtown Mackinac Island taken from Fort Mackinac shows a thriving fishing village with five docks, warehouse fish equipment, some impressive private houses, and many of what were called "shanties." Some of the more significant features are:

    a) Indian teepees and canoes on the beach.
    b) Wendell's. Jacob Wendell was custom house collector. He also operated a general store and supplied lake steamers with cordwood for their boilers. Note the fish net dryer at the end of his building. Later the site of the Chippewa Hotel.
    c) Hoban dock, operated by John and James Hoban. They also dealt in cordwood. Later the dock was acquired by George T. Arnold, who operated the principal ferry line to the mainland, but at this time it was used for commercial fishing purposes.
    d) Bennett dock.
    e) Lasley dock, built by James Lasley, who was an early Island postmaster. It also was used to supply wood.
    f) Biddle dock, owned by Edward Biddle, who also dealt in fish and wood.
    g) Biddle storehouse. Note the fish net dryer. Later the Palmer House hotel was built here.
    h) Mackinac House hotel.
    i) Murray Hotel.
    j) Northern Hotel. Later to be remodelled and known as Fenton's Indian Bazaar.

4. This is the earliest photograph taken from one of the docks and dates from 1865. Wendell's (The "W" is missing.) is on the right. Across the street are the Northern Hotel and a large warehouse, later the site of the Island's drugstore. On the extreme left is the Mackinac House, which was operated by John Becher and his wife, Justine. In 1860 his guests included a schoolteacher, a fish inspector, and a cooper. These hotels are strictly food and lodging — no large porches that are so common later.

1

2

3

4

5

6

1. Dock warehouses were used to store fish after they had been sorted, packed, and salted. Mackinac Island was the principal processing and shipping center for fishing grounds up to 150 miles away. Most sought-after fish were the lake trout and whitefish. Note the way in which the original center building was enlarged by adding sheds.

2. Hoists that were affixed directly to the dock made it easier to load the fish barrels on the steamers which made scheduled stops at Mackinac on their way to Buffalo, Detroit, and Chicago.

3. A fish storage and processing building (a) is close to one of the docks. Fish were taken mostly with cotton gill nets, so-called because as the fish attempted to swim through they were caught by their gills. Fishermen in Mackinac boats lifted miles of nets daily. The net drying rack is adjacent to the building.

4. The United States Customs agent, Jacob Wendell, lived and worked in this house. He was a long-time Island resident prominent in fishing and commerce. In 1870 Mackinac County (which included more than the Island) led all others with 59 fisheries employing 167 men, who earned $17,000. There was $54,000 in capital invested. Over 10,000 barrels of fish were shipped at a value of $103,000 that year.

5. The Northern Hotel was interesting for a number of reasons. It was a very old building in 1870 and apparently of log construction. The three visible gables indicate that some of the guests slept upstairs, and the poor spacing indicates the gables were added after the building became a hotel. The boards nailed to the roof were to aid firemen in case of a chimney fire. This building will appear many times in later photographs. An elderly resident said in 1936 that this building dated from 1810.

6. This is hardly the kind of building to enhance its neighboring four-star Northern Hotel. It is, however, a typical square frame building of Mackinac. As with others, the need for more room was satisfied by adding a lean-to — in this case, two of them. This do-it-yourself architecture resulted in the quaint salt-box houses with their long, sloping roof lines.

7. This 1870 photograph, which was taken from the east bluff, shows the growing congestion of houses in the village. The *Magnet,* a wood-burning sidewheeler, is tied up along one of the five docks. Stacks of wood for fueling its boilers are piled neatly where the boat crews can easily load them. The Stuart House (a), flanked by the old American Fur Warehouse and the Clerks' Quarters, has been converted to a hotel and is now operated by Eliza McLeod. The Indian Dormitory (b) has been leased to the village for a school, and the Island children will trudge up the walk between the picket fences for the next eighty-five years. In the foreground is the Indian Agency house (c) with its additions built on additions. Note particularly the bark roof and the privy, sometimes called the "necessary" house. This is the last known picture of the Agency, as it burned to the ground in 1873.

1

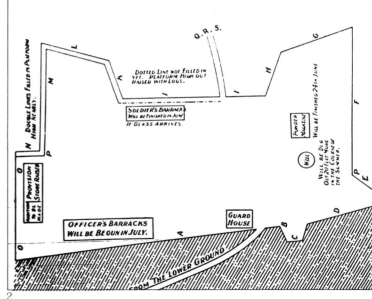

2

1. Fort Mackinac has dominated the history of Mackinac Island. Behind its limestone walls, hundreds of soldiers have served their king and country. Perhaps to signify its important role, Davis in his 1839 watercolor pictured extraordinarily large American colors on the garrison flagpole.

2. The general outlines of the bastions and key structures were sketched soon after construction began in 1780. This plan was copied from the now lost original by a late 19th century researcher. It shows the original placement of the guardhouse, officers' barracks, provision store, soldiers' barracks, powder magazine, and well. Of these only the limestone officers' barracks remain today.

3. This drawing by Private W. Brenschutz, Company I, Fifth Infantry, in 1842 shows how the Americans had greatly enlarged the fort to accommodate two companies of infantry:

    a) South Sally Port
    b) Guardhouse
    c) Officers' Wood Quarters (Canteen)
    d) Officers' Stone Quarters
    e) West Blockhouse
    f) Hospital
    g) Commanding Officer's House
    h) North Blockhouse
    i) Soldiers' Barracks
    j) Mess hall and kitchen
    k) Blacksmith Shop
    l) North Sally Port
    m) Quartermaster Storehouse
    n) Post Headquarters
    o) Ordnance and Powder Magazine
    p) East Blockhouse

4. An unknown military artist sketched this elevation of Fort Mackinac looking west toward the mainland in 1874. Most of the buildings are horizontal log and frame construction and covered with weatherboards:

    a) Sentry box. The soldier to the right is standing over the South Sally Port. This is at the top of the long ramp leading down the bluff to town.
    b) Guardhouse
    c) Officers' Wood Quarters
    d) Officers' Stone Quarters. The only building remaining from the British era, and the only one built entirely of limestone.
    e) West Blockhouse. From the early American period. Constructed of limestone and mortar with a squared-timber second story.
    f) Post Hospital. Provision store formerly located on this site.
    g) Commanding Officer's House
    h) North Blockhouse. Limestone and squared timber construction.
    i) Soldiers' Barracks. The largest building in the fort and at the north side of the parade ground. Three barracks were built on this site, the latest in 1859. One non-commissioned officer lived on the west end.
    j) Blacksmith Shop. Later this shop was moved to the soldiers' garden area below the fort.
    k) North Sally Port. Tradition says at this spot the Americans surrendered Fort Mackinac on July 17, 1812. It leads to the rifle range and barn areas.
    l) Quartermaster Storehouse
    m) Post Headquarters
    n) Ordnance storage and Powder Magazine. Later the site of the Commissary. The post well, which supposedly was dug to a depth of 150 feet, is just to the left. Archaeologists are very anxious to excavate the well because it is likely full of trash and other most interesting 19th century relics. Not shown because it is to the back of the artist is the East Blockhouse.

5. In this 1874 picture taken from the same vantage point as sketch, the garrison is lined up for morning inspection — or more likely to have its picture taken by a pioneering photographer.

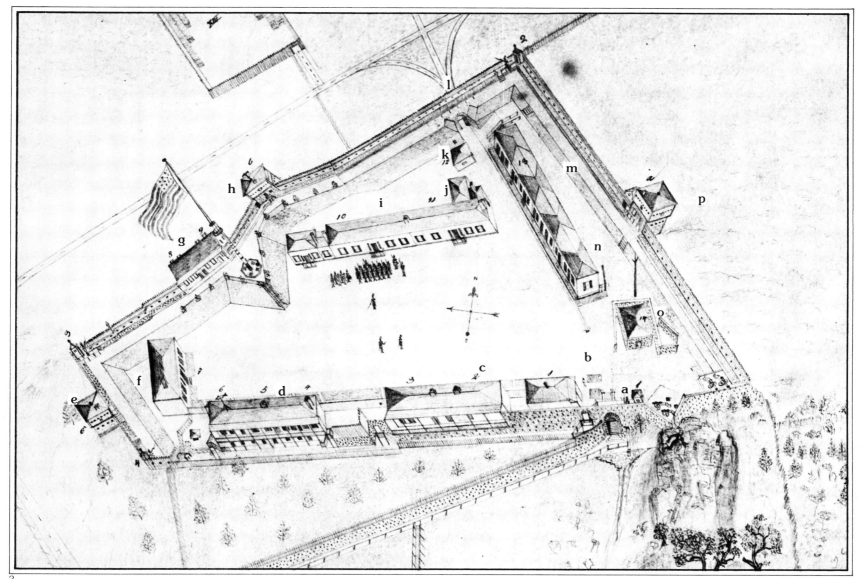

3

William L. Clements Library

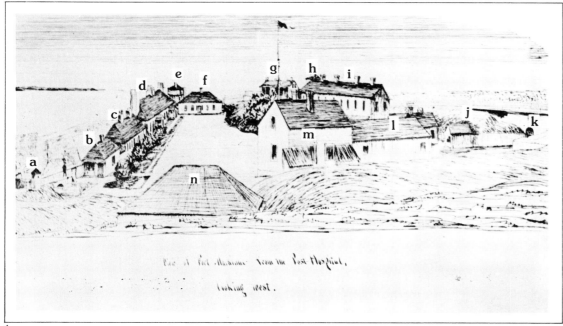

Line at Fort Mackinac from the Post Hospital,

looking west.

4

National Archives

5

Clarke Historical Library

1

2

3

4

5

6

Clarke Historical Library

1. Mackinac Island is composed primarily of limestone. Not only can the stone be used for construction, but when the rock is "burnt," the resulting mortar makes a good bond to hold the stones together. This limestone kiln for making "lime," located a quarter of a mile from the fort, was used by the soldiers.

2. The officers' stone quarters is one of the buildings that remains from the British period. Its stone construction makes it unique among the fort buildings, although in the first story of the three blockhouses and in the fort's retaining walls the native limestone was also used. Some of the walls measure eight feet in thickness, so it could stand quite a pounding from enemy artillery. In 1814, while the American ships were anchored in the Straits before their ill-fated attack, the British used the basement of this building for a refuge for the Island's women and children.

3. The soldiers' barracks built in 1859 and shown in this late 19th century photograph was the third to be built on the site. Private quarters for married soldiers were on either end. The second story housed the chapel for many years. In 1883 two companies of men lived here.

4. Maintenance was a constant problem for the fort commanders. Note in this 1870 photograph that the center retaining wall is made of vertical log pickets held by embedded horizontal logs.

5. This hospital building dates from 1828 after the original British-built structure was torn down.

6. The officers' wood quarters (center) was built in 1835. This old log building now covered with siding was the army home of many United States officers until 1894. Perhaps the most distinguished tenants not in the Federal service were three Confederate prisoners, Generals William G. Harding and Washington Barrows, and Judge Joseph C. Guild from Tennessee. They arrived on the steamer *Illinois* in May, 1862 and remained in confinement under Michigan's Stanton Guards militia until transferred to Johnson's Island in Lake Erie that fall.

7. Originally the commissary storehouse was in the garden area below the fort, but in 1879 this building was constructed on the site of the old magazine. The fort well is just to the right of the commissary.

8. The west blockhouse is probably the most photographed building in Fort Mackinac. When this picture was taken in 1900, a hundred years after construction, the top story showed signs of wear. The small holes in both stories are musket firing portals.

9. In the 1840's Mackinac was one of several midwestern forts where army personnel were assigned for their tours of duty. "My company," wrote Lt. John C. Pemberton of Pennsylvania in 1840, "has been ordered to the Island of Mackinac, the very northern point of Michigan, much to my discontent." However, in his year at Fort Mackinac he made the best of the situation. According to tradition, the young Lieutenant became greatly enamored with Sophia, a local beauty and the daughter of Edward Biddle. However, when he found her mother was of Indian descent, he broke off the romance. After leaving Mackinac and marrying a Virginia girl, he joined the Confederate Army when the Civil War broke out in 1861. Whether the Sophia Biddle story is true or not, history will remember General John C. Pemberton as having the dubious distinction of surrendering Vicksburg to General U. S. Grant.

7

8

9

1

2

History Division, Michigan Department of State

5

Clarke Historical Library

6

1. The uniform worn when this photograph was taken had been adopted before the Civil War and was based on a French design. The wool jacket is navy blue; the trousers, light blue. The hat or kepi was standard until the late 1870's. Rank is indicated by the stripe on the non-commissioned officers' trousers and by the sleeve stripes. Pay for enlisted men was $13 a month for privates, $15 for corporals, and $17 to $34 for the various grades of sergeants.

2. Life at the fort became, if not more enjoyable, at least more comfortable after 1881, when Quartermaster Lt. Dwight H. Kelton devised a central water supply system. The water was pumped up the hill from a spring and into a tank installed in the second story of the north blockhouse (right). Then it flowed through pipes by gravity to all the garrison buildings. For a hundred years the fort's water had been supplied by a water wagon pulled manually from the not-too-reliable wells or up the 130-foot bluff.

3. In addition to the water system, Kelton's contributions include a good history of the Mackinac region which he called, "Annals of Fort Mackinac." First published in 1883, it went through several editions.

Clarke Historical Library

3   4   7

8

History Division, Michigan Department of State

4. The principal roadway to Fort Mackinac from the village was cut in the hill west of the stockaded fort. In this 1870 picture the soldiers appear to be taking a break from their fence construction project.

5. For every soldier who managed to find a little romance on Mackinac Island, there were a hundred who faced boredom, endless drill, and some very cold and long winters. A few of the soldiers brought their wives with them, but low army pay and poor living conditions made it necessary for the women to work as laundresses or cleaning women in order to survive. In 1860 Private Martin Chubb and his wife, Anna, shared quarters in the soldiers' barracks with 51 members of Company G of the 2nd Artillery. Sgt. William Marshall and his wife, Fanny, were lucky to be assigned a small private house in the fort, but they needed it for their eight children. Here a toddler holds her father's hand near the north sally port in 1874.

6. When these soldiers lined up on the parade, one non-commissioned officer's son was included on the left.

7. The officers, of course, fared better. Captain Henry Pratt and wife, Mary, occupied the large and comfortable commanding officer's house that was built in 1835. The couple had two servants to help keep the house clean and bring up their six children. Lieutenants Henry Smalley and George Hartseff shared the officers' stone quarters and had their own private stairway down the bluff. Here two officers escort their ladies down the steps while a fellow soldier waits at the gate below.

8. Then, a walk through the woods was always fun — especially when accompanied by a lady. This chaperoned couple is approaching Sugar Loaf.

1

2

1. A young girl stands at the turnstile at the bottom of the ramp to Fort Mackinac. The turnstile was necessary to discourage cows from detouring to the fort on their way to pasture.

2. Drills and parades were daily occurrences at Fort Mackinac. Here a company of the 10th Infantry stands early morning inspection in 1882. Wives and children observe from the hillside in front of the north blockhouse. The commanding officer lived in the house on the left. This uniform was adopted by the army in 1872, but not widely used until the early 1880's. The unusual spiked helmets were copied from the Prussian Army, which was held in high esteem after its crushing defeat of France in 1871.

3. The enlisted men used the south sally port ramp to town and to their gardens. This 1888 picture shows the partially completed Trinity Episcopal Church at the left. The tents in the background constitute a summer military encampment.

4. Guard duty is part of the soldiers' work, and at Mackinac, although the view may have been more spectacular than at other army posts, the job was just as tedious. Here a post Civil War soldier stands before his sentry box while a comrade blows a call from the lower gun platform.

5. The armament consisted mostly of light artillery. This Civil War vintage six-pounder cannon is mounted on a field carriage.

6. There were usually several pieces on the upper gun platform.

7. This monstrous seige mortar was brought to Fort Mackinac after the Civil War.

3

6

History Division, Michigan Department of State

7

Clarke Historical Library

1

2

History Division, Michigan Department of State

8

3

4

5

6

38

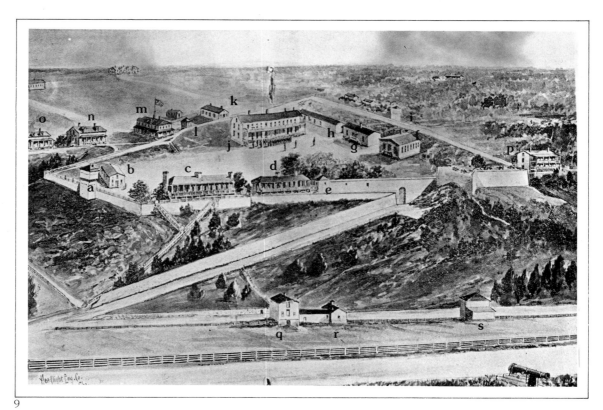

9

1. The soldiers' food at Fort Mackinac was not much different from that at other army posts. The government provided pork and beef which was usually boiled or made into stew or hash. Dried beans and hard tack also were shipped in while the boats were running. Most other food stuffs were purchased either locally or through the commissary. At Mackinac vegetables were grown in soldier-attended gardens. This 1874 sketch shows the gardens below the fort. On the left is the granary, and on the right, the animal barn.

2. Although the growing season was very short, the garden produced a variety of vegetables which included cabbage, potatoes, leeks, carrots, radishes, onions and cucumbers. Also, the soldiers harvested apples, cherries, strawberries and currants. Sometime in the 1880's a wagon shed was added to the granary, and the blacksmith moved his operations to the small building with the chimney and window.

3. This view from the bluff shows the well-traveled road to the blacksmith and wagon shed. The garden is enclosed by a fence which discouraged most children and all cattle. Something has happened to the granary, as all that remains is the foundation.

4. Fences had to be high and substantial to keep the cattle out of the gardens. No doubt as they made their way up fort hill from the village barns to the pasture, they cast a longing eye at the soldiers' corn field.

5. The cows and horses were kept in this barn, but were pastured during the day west of the fort with Islanders' cattle in the "government pasture."

6. An unknown artist painted this view of the fort barns late in the army occupation.

7. The government pasture.

8. The view from Fort Mackinac was spectacular. If the enemy came from the west, south, or east, he could be spotted ten miles away. Visibility was not so good to the north, and, as we have already seen, that was the way the British came in 1812. But by 1875 the English were resigned to the permanent loss of Mackinac, the Indians were quiet, and this soldier is probably looking only to see what is going on downtown.

9. In 1895 military life at Fort Mackinac came to an end. The United States found that the old fort was no longer suitable as a garrison for its troops. The British and Indian threat which had been the main reason for garrisoning this post was no longer real. The old buildings which had housed English and American troops since 1780 were too antiquated for 20th century soldiers. Shortly after the last company marched down the ramp to take up residence in another fort, the entire complex was offered to the State of Michigan for park purposes. This "bird's eye" sketch made by an unknown artist shows one of the final inspections before the soldiers' barracks. It also shows in slightly distorted perspective the principal military structures at that time:

a) West Blockhouse
b) Hospital
c) Officers' Stone Quarters
d) Officers' Wood Quarters
e) Guardhouse
f) Commissary
g) Post Headquarters
h) Quartermaster Storehouse
i) East Blockhouse
j) Soldiers' Barracks
k) Schoolhouse
l) North Blockhouse
m) Commanding Officer's House
n) Major's House
o) Captain's House
p) Surgeon's Quarters
q) Granary
r) Blacksmith Shop
s) Animal Barn

THE VISITORS

In the 1880's the livelihood of the people changed from the processing of natural resources to a service-oriented economy dependent on the Island's summer visitors. Just as the decline in fur-bearing animals had ended Astor's Mackinac empire a half century earlier, over fishing, as reflected in sharply lower catches of lake trout and whitefish, put the skids under the commercial fish industry in northern Michigan. The local French, Indian, and Irish residents stopped making barrels, put away their nets, and turned to providing the services demanded by vacationing America.

With the new economy came a change in the physical appearance of Mackinac Island. The docks were improved to accommodate large excursion ships. Many of the old shanties were torn down to make room for shops and stores. The hotels were renovated to provide furnishings the Victorian traveler would appreciate. Like a young lady getting ready for a special date, the Island began to take on a fresh look.

This is not to say that tourism was entirely new to Mackinac Island. Actually, since the 1820's people had been coming for short visits, and many were impressed with the Island's charm and climate. The distinguished author Thomas McKenney, after a visit in 1826, wrote, "Mackinac is really worth seeing. There is no finer climate in the world." He predicted it would become a fashionable summer resort. Charles Lanman in his *Summer in the Wilderness* published in 1847 said, "It is indeed one of the most unique and delightful places in the world." He, too, believed that, because of its picturesque scenery and the "toxic character" of its climate, it was destined to be one of the most attractive watering places in the country.

Perhaps the greatest publicity came from the English writer Harriet Martineau. Born in 1802, she was one of the phenomena of her age — a woman who traveled widely and wrote about her experiences in a readable and lively way. In 1836 Miss Martineau visited the United States and, shortly after, wrote her *Retrospect of Western Travel,* which was an immediate success. While she was on the Island, she visited the Presbyterian Mission, observed Mackinac's "chief curiosities," discussed Indian legends with Henry Schoolcraft, and visited the fort, where an officer told her Mackinac had nine months of winter and three months of cool weather but was so healthy that a person had to get off the Island to die. Her visit was a resounding success, and she advised her readers that Mackinac was "the wildest and tenderest piece of beauty that I have yet viewed on God's earth."

But, until after 1870, these visitors to Mackinac were the exception rather than the rule. Travel was a luxury and an adventure reserved for the hardy or the very rich. Most Americans got their thrills of discovery second hand through the eyes of one who had been there.

All that was to change. The industrialization of America produced a well-to-do class, many of whom chose to travel and to spend their summers in a relaxing and healthy environment. The frontier, which had been a very real barrier since colonial days, was pushed so far west that suddenly it was no longer an obstacle for travel. Steamboat lines began to vie for customers as they connected the growing industrial cities and the Great Lakes. The railroads also pushed their tracks steadily northward and offered stiff competition for the lake excursion boats. Mackinac Island was a principal stop for both the Cleveland and Chicago boat lines, and, when the Michigan Central Railroad reached Mackinaw City in 1881, the Island was less than an hour's ferry ride from the mainland.

The late 19th century tourist was a new breed. Unlike Miss Martineau and her fellow travelers of the 1820's and 1830's who expected to rough it in such a remote area and were satisfied with modest hotel accommodations, the new visitors demanded much more. Those who could afford to travel in the 1880's could afford to travel in luxury. They came prepared to spend the summer, bringing wives, children, in-laws and a full complement of servants to help move innumerable steamer trunks from the dock to their summer quarters.

Serving these Victorian visitors, then, was the challenge faced by Mackinac Islanders. These summer transplants had to be housed, wined, dined, transported, entertained, amused, amazed, enlightened and, in all those activities, photographed!

1. From the first Indians who paddled their canoes across the four miles that separated it from the mainland, to the passengers of the luxurious Great Lakes excursion boats who made it a port of call, the visitors have come in ever increasing numbers to breathe the fresh air, discover the scenic vistas, explore the geological formations and absorb the historic charm of the Island.

The principal line to serve Mackinac from Detroit and lake sites east was the Detroit and Cleveland Steam Navigation Company. Although it operated locally in Lake Erie and the Detroit River as early as 1850, it was not until 1882 that its modern boats began to make regular trips to Mackinac Island. Its fleet included the *City of Alpena* and *City of Mackinac*. Mackinac has never suffered for lack of visitors.

2. This advertisement appeared in local newspapers in 1863. The steam packets, *Meteor* and *Illinois*, stopped at Mackinac Island on their way to Lake Superior.

3. The 300-foot long *City of Mackinac*, shown approaching the Island in 1895, cost $350,000 and carried a crew of fifty.

4. The steamboats burned wood, and the stop at Mackinac Island also meant refueling. Here a load of chopped wood on the principal town dock waits the arrival of the next excursion boat.

5. The *Northwest* and her sister ship, the *Northland*, were the show passenger steamers on the Great Lakes. Built by James Hill to promote the development of the Northwest, they plied between Buffalo and Chicago to Duluth. Reports E. W. Puttkammer of Mackinac Island, who as a child observed many arrivals and departures: *"I remember that, when the ship left Mackinac Island, it did so in a theatrical manner. The first officer stood by the passenger gangplank near the stern and, as the moment of departure approached, he would hold his watch in one hand, look intently at it, and then, a few seconds before the time, he would raise the other hand and, at the very moment when the time to leave had come, he would drop it, the gangplank would be brought aboard, and the ship would depart. All of it, of course, for show, but it certainly was an effective pageant."*

6. Meals were served in this spacious lounge. Lake travel had certainly come a long way from the time the Indians paddled their canoes over these waters. No doubt the artist who painted the mural at the end of the room had this thought in mind.

7. Fashionable wicker chairs, Persian rugs, writing desks with a few reference books and fine wood paneling along the ample passageway would satisfy the most meticulous Victorian traveler.

8. The D & C boats were the latest word in comfort and convenience. It was no idle boast that they were "floating hotels." They claimed 150 staterooms and parlors furnished with, among other things, "wire and hair mattresses."

9. Not all staterooms had couches and writing desks. Here is a more austere cabin. Notice the photographer's camera reflected in the mirror.

10. It took a large crew to run an excursion boat. The boiler room boys assembled on the main dock for this group picture in 1910.

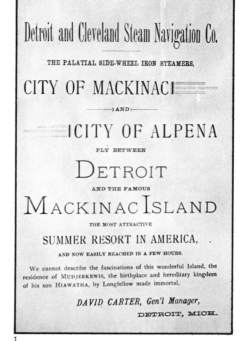

1

2

5

6

8

4

8

9

Clarke Historical Library

10

1

1. One of the most famous ferries was the *Algomah,* shown here approaching the dock in 1894. Its engines were installed personally by young Henry Ford of Detroit. Many years later, when the vessel was scrapped, the engines were removed and turned over to Ford.

2. The *Northland* and *Tionesta* were tied up in the harbor when this 1910 photograph was taken.

3. The *J. T. Wing,* one of the last sailing vessels on the Great Lakes, passes Mackinac Island with a load of wood. The vessel later was used as a maritime museum at Detroit's Belle Isle.

4. After the railroad reached Mackinaw City in 1881, the Arnold Transit Company began to ferry tourists from the mainland. Here the coal-burning *Chippewa* enters Mackinac harbor in 1910.

5. The *Eugene C. Hart* is docked at Mackinac Island harbor in 1900. Note the second vessel approaching is using both steam and sail.

6. The iron-hulled *Michigan* made stops at Mackinac Island.

7. Richard P. Hulbert noted on August 15, 1888 the vessel anchored briefly in the harbor while en route to Milwaukee.

5

3

(U.S. Steamer Michigan)

The United States Man of War Michigan dropped anchor in the harbor on Thursday afternoon. The Ship is under orders to report to the Commander in Chief of the "Grand Army of the Republic" at Milwaukee, and will represent the Navy at the National Encampment to be held in that City, and is specially fitted and manned for her duty— The Old Ship will be the most interesting thing, the Old Soldiers will find in or about Milwaukee— You all know that she was built in 1844, or rather that she was built in Pittsburgh, and put together and launched in Erie Penn— in the year mentioned. She has been in continuous Service on the Lakes ever since, though frozen fast in her slip three months out of every twelve— She was the first Iron Ship on Fresh Water— The Michigan is our only Naval Vessel on the Northern Frontier, and though she may be an Ancient Ship, with Ancient Artillery, she is sufficient protection against the Barbarians who infest just "beyont" our Northern Line fence— The note improvements in the Old Ship

7

4

6

1

2

Grand Rapids & Indiana Ry

THE FAVORITE LINE TO

MACKINAC ISLAND

AND ALL OTHER

NORTHERN MICHIGAN

SUMMER RESORTS

During the Summer months solid vestibuled trains are operated with through Pullman Sleeping Cars and Dining Cars from

CINCINNATI   INDIANAPOLIS
LOUISVILLE   ST. LOUIS
CHICAGO   DETROIT
and GRAND RAPIDS, to the North.

Send two-cent stamp for beautiful illustrated booklet

"MICHIGAN IN SUMMER"

a descriptive of all the famous Northern Michigan Summer Resorts, and containing 200 photographs, list of hotels, maps, and other interesting information, to

C. L. LOCKWOOD, G. P. & T. A.

3

4

1. In 1887 John Cudahy's black yacht *Idler* is tied up at the right. The small shed in the foreground is a blacksmith shop owned by the Arnold Transit Company. Of the four ferry boats at the main dock only the second from the left is identifiable as the *Ossifrage.*

2. Sometimes there was nowhere to put the passengers. In the 1880's a popular run was the Inland Waterway route. Boats like the *Algoma Central,* pictured here, carried short-stay visitors from Charlevoix and Petoskey to Mackinac Island. After a brief stop, they left for Cheboygan, where they transferred to a smaller boat which took them through Burt, Mullet and Crooked Lakes to Conway, where a stagecoach brought them the rest of the way back to Petoskey.

3. In 1881 the railroad reached Mackinaw City and the lake boats had considerable competition. The Grand Rapids and Indiana offered passage from Chicago to the Straits for $16.80 round trip and from Detroit for $15.70.

4. Private motor yachts from Chicago, Detroit and Cleveland also brought visitors to the Island. In this 1910 photograph, three such vessels are anchored in the harbor.

5. If you could afford it, this was the way to come. A private yacht with your own crew and, out on the sun deck, comfortable wicker chairs, an expensive Persian rug and a vase of flowers.

6. The excursion boats could compete with the railroads, but the automobile and freeways sounded the death knell for the large lake boats. By 1968 the *North American* and *South American,* built in 1913 and 1914, respectively, and operated by the Georgian Bay Line were sold, and the era ended.

5

6

Robert Benjamin

47

1

MISSION HOUSE,

MACKINAC, MICHIGAN.

E. A. FRANKS, Proprietor.

———•———

This old and Favorite Hotel is delightfully
situated adjoining the

✦ *National Park* ✦

ON THE

Romantic Island of Mackinac,

Within a short distance of the Arched Rock,
Sugar Loaf, Giant's Causway, and other
natural curiosities in which this
famed Island abounds.

Good Accommodations for 200 Guests.

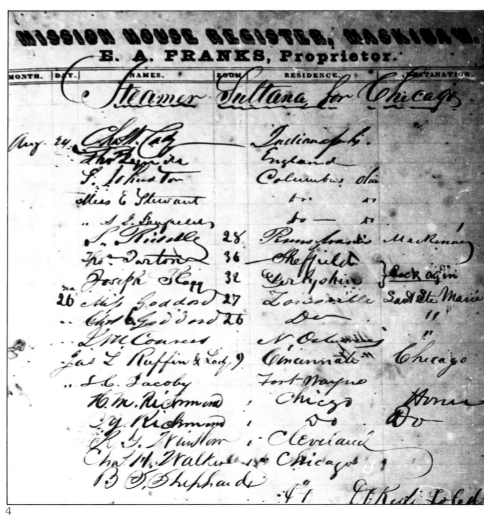

4

2

Minnesota Historical Society

MISSION HOUSE,

MACKINAC, MICH.,

E. A. FRANKS, Proprietor.

———•◆•———

This old and favorite HOTEL is most delightfully situated on the romantic ISLAND OF MACKINAC, within a short distance of the water's edge, and contiguous to the Arched Rock, Sugar Loaf, and other Natural Curiosities in which this famed Island abounds; being alike celebrated for its pure air, romantic scenery, and fishing grounds.

MACKINAC, *July*, 1862.

3

5

1. There was no doubt Mackinac Island was a healthful spot: All the doctors said it was. In 1870 Dr. H. R. Mills, post surgeon at Fort Mackinac, advised Rev. Van Fleet, "No better place can be found for chlerotic girls and puny boys, worn out men and women, whether suffering from overworked brain or muscle." And he added, "Bowel complaints seldom prevail" here. One unnamed doctor quoted in a Grand Rapids and Indiana Railroad brochure said that the Island air was "beneficial to those who suffer from nervous prostration and debilitating effects of heat and malaria." This was confirmed by one devotee in 1897, "It must be air that came from Eden and escaped the curse." The homes of most visitors who came to spend the summer months at Mackinac Island were the Victorian hotels.

2. The Mission House was one of the oldest Island hotels. Formerly used by a Presbyterian missionary society from Massachusetts to house and train Indian children, it was acquired by Edward A. Franks and converted to hotel purposes in 1852. By 1860 Franks had a staff of eighteen, including thirteen black servants. He valued his property at $5,000, which made it one of the most valuable pieces of real estate on Mackinac Island.

3. One disadvantage of the Mission House was its distance from down town, as it was located at the extreme east end of the village. Perhaps for this reason it was known for its "quiet repose." But, as this 1862 advertisement notes, it was close to the natural curiosities of the Island.

4. All guests signed the Mission House register. On August 24 and 26, 1852, these people were off the Steamer *Sultana,* an 800-ton sidewheeler that ran between Buffalo and Chicago.

5. In 1900 Island photographer William H. Gardiner took this picture of the Mission House staff.

Chicago Historical Society

1

ISLAND HOUSE

MACKINAC ISLAND, MICH.

THE ISLAND HOUSE is beautifully situat[ed]
on Elevated Ground fronting the wat[er]
a pleasant distance from the Village a[nd]
Steamboat Landing.

Carriages always in attendance to conv[ey]
Guests to and from the House.

GOOD ACCOMMODATIONS FOR 150 GUESTS.

Captain H. VAN ALLEN,
PROPRIET[OR]

2

3

5

1. Located a quarter mile closer to the docks, the Island House was built in 1852 by Charles O'Malley and for years rivaled the Mission House as one of Mackinac's favorite hotels. It was, according to an 1862 advertisement, designed "for the entertainment of travelers, pleasure parties, invalids and others who desire a comfortable home while seeking pleasure and health."

2. In the 90's a west wing was added (to the right of the sail) which made it possible to increase accommodations for guests from 150 to 300. The house on the extreme right was occupied by the Chicago meat packer, Philip D. Armour, and his family.

3. By 1900 a large east wing in the architectural style of a southern plantation home housed a dining room. Rates were $3 a day with discounts for extended visits. Patrons spoke approvingly of the comfortable quarters and well maintained grounds.

4. In 1910 it would have been safe to call the Island House a family hotel. Just about every age group is represented here as the guests cluster on the porch for picture taking. The sharply attired gentleman under the kerosene lamp looks strangely modern. Note the black household servant at right center.

5. Also on the east end was the St. Cloud Hotel furnished "in the Queen Anne style" and featuring a "famous string band."

4

SAINT CLOUD HOTEL,
MACKINAC ISLAND, MICHIGAN.

SITUATED upon beautifully terraced grounds overlooking the Harbor and Straits of Mackinac. Is complete and Modern in all its appointments and furnished in the Queen-Anne Style.

THE SAINT CLOUD HOTEL offers inducements to Tourists and Pleasure-Seekers that are unsurpassed. Its corps of colored servants is the best while its Culinary department is under the charge of a "Chef de Cuisine" engaged at great expense.

Its elegant broad verandas, its large, airy, well-ventilated rooms, its Operatic Singers, and its

FAMOUS STRING BAND

are attractions by which this Hotel has gained its world-wide reputation and which no one can disregard in the selection of a home-like stopping place while sojourning on this lovely and romantic Isle.

WENDELL & McDONALD, Managers.

1. In the main part of town there were three well patronized hostelries. The New Murray (a), Mackinac House (b), and, on the extreme left, the Palmer House operated by Louis and Lenore Jolie. This 1882 picture shows some of the Palmer's patrons sitting on the porch (and on the road) waiting for something to happen. In the meantime, the cook in his white apron is figuring out how many plates for supper.

2. The Mackinac House at the head of the main dock was rebuilt after fire burned it to the ground in 1887. William C. Hulbert noted in his diary that the fire broke out "between 4 and 5 o'clock A.M." on February 1. Not only the hotel, but the neighboring Highstone store, Chambers building and Dominic Murray's store also were lost in the catastrophe. The new building was called appropriately "The New Mackinac." In 1938 it was purchased by the City, torn down and the site turned into the small park which remains today.

3. Advertisements need not be dull, said Proprietor Emerick in 1895. His rates ranged from $2.50 to $3.00 a day. The hotel was particularly popular with transients, partly because it was only a step away from where the steamboats docked.

4. Next door was a competitor, "The New Murray." Like all hotels of its day, the Murray had a large porch where you could visit with your fellow guests, complain about the service and brag about how many summers you had been coming to Mackinac. Hacks (carriages for hire) are parked close by, and the hotel even had a general merchandise and gift store in the building. No doubt about it, if you wanted to be in the middle of things, "The New Murray" was for you.

5. Further west along Main Street, as already noted, was the Palmer House, where informality was the order of the day when this picture was taken.

6. Another smaller Island hotel was the Lozon House, owned by Josef Lozon. He came to Mackinac Island before the War of 1812 to work as a *voyageur* for the Northwest and American Fur Company. Hulbert noted that Lozon died January 2, 1888 "of gangrene at the age of 91." That may be he standing in the doorway about to ring the dinner bell. There seems to be some sort of picture exhibit on the porch. When Henry Hamilton of Chicago stayed here in 1878, he said that Indians came into the hotel selling small birch bark canoes and mococks of maple sugar.

7. At the extreme west end of town you could stay at the Lakeview for $2.50 and $3.00 a night. The old Lakeview was built in 1858 by Reuben Chapman near the Lozon House. In 1880 it was purchased by C. C. Cable, who with his son operated it for many years. By 1901 it was greatly enlarged by adding two wings.

1   Clarke Historical

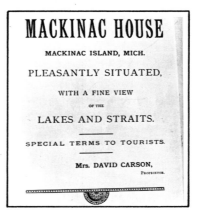

MACKINAC HOUSE

MACKINAC ISLAND, MICH.

PLEASANTLY SITUATED,

WITH A FINE VIEW

OF THE

LAKES AND STRAITS.

SPECIAL TERMS TO TOURISTS.

Mrs. DAVID CARSON,
PROPRIETOR.

7

THE NEW MACKINA

2

5

100 GOOD ROOMS

Built upon the site of the 'Mackinac House,' which was burned in January, 1887.

The New Mackinac

FRED. R. EMERICK,
PROPRIETOR AND MANAGER.

Mackinae Island, Mieh.

THIS HOUSE IS WELL ARRANGED FOR THE COMFORT OF TOURISTS, AND IS CONVENIENTLY LOCATED ON THE LAKE FRONT, AND ONE HUNDRED FEET FROM THE D.&C.N.CO'S PASSENGER WHARF. THE FURNITURE, CARPETS, ETC. ARE ALL NEW. THE HOUSE IS EQUIPPED WITH ELECTRIC BELLS, HOT& COLD WATER BATHS, AND MODERN CONVENIENCES.

SAVE HACK HIRE TO AND FROM YOUR HOTEL

THIS HOTEL was built for the special comfort of summer boarders.
On arrival, each guest will be asked how he likes the situation, and if he says the hotel ought to have been placed on Fort Holmes or on Round Island, the location of the hotel will be immediately changed.

Corner front rooms up one flight for every guest. Gas, electricity, hot and cold water, laundry; telegraph, restaurant, fire alarm, bar room, billiard table, sewing machine, piano, and all modern conveniences in every room. Meals every minute, consequently no second table. French and German dictionaries furnished every guest to make up such a bill of fare as he may desire.

Waiters of any nationality or color desired. Every waiter furnished with a fan, button-hole bouquet, full dress suit, ball tablet and his hair parted in the middle.

Every guest will have the best seat in the dining hall and the best waiter in the house.

Our clerk was specially educated for "The New Mackinac," he wears the original Koh-i-nor diamond, and is prepared to please everybody. He is always ready to sing any song, play any musical instrument, match worsted, take a hand at draw poker, play billiards, "see a friend," loan his eye-glasses, sharpen your pencil, get the cinder out of your eye, take you out rowing, lead the german, amuse the children, make a fourth at whist, or flirt with any young lady, and will not mind being cut dead when Pa comes down. He will attend to the telephone and answer all questions in Choctaw, Chinese, Chippewa, Volapuk, or any other of the court languages of Europe.

The proprietor will always be happy to hear that some other hotel is "the best in the country." Special attention given to parties who give information as to "how these things are done in Boston."

3

6

53

1. Nearby was the Windermere. No doubt its ornate scrollwork and balconies upon balconies were designed to make the Victorian traveler feel at home in the 1890's.

2. Across the street from the Windermere was the Iroquois. Originally built as a home for Robert Benjamin in 1903, it was soon sold to Samuel Poole, the former superintendent of the State Park, who enlarged it in 1907 and operated it as a hotel for many years.

3. The Grand Central, which is presently called Windsor, was located just off Market Street and directly across from Ste. Ann's, the first location of the Catholic Church which Sinclair moved to Mackinac Island in 1780.

4. One of the earliest Mackinac Island hotels was located on Market Street. First operated as the McLeod House in the early 1860's, the former buildings of the American Fur Company were admirably suited for summer visitors. Ronald McLeod, however, could not make it go and in 1870 offered the buildings, including two parlors, office, seventy sleeping rooms, barber shop, laundry, bath room, horse, cow, buggy, dray, harnesses and sleigh for $6,000. The new owners joined the buildings with the three-tiered porch shown in this 1895 photograph and changed the name to capitalize on the history of the structures. In 1930 the property was sold to the City of Mackinac Island for $8,000.

1

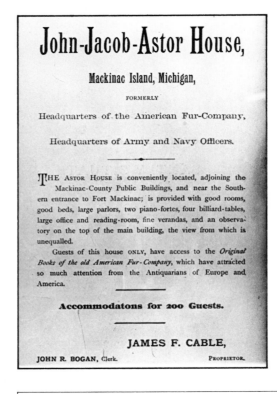

John-Jacob-Astor House,

Mackinac Island, Michigan,

FORMERLY

Headquarters of the American Fur-Company,

Headquarters of Army and Navy Officers.

THE ASTOR HOUSE is conveniently located, adjoining the Mackinac-County Public Buildings, and near the Southern entrance to Fort Mackinac; is provided with good rooms, good beds, large parlors, two piano-fortes, four billiard-tables, large office and reading-room, fine verandas, and an observatory on the top of the main building, the view from which is unequalled.

Guests of this house ONLY, have access to the *Original Books of the old American Fur-Company*, which have attracted so much attention from the Antiquarians of Europe and America.

Accommodatons for 200 Guests.

JAMES F. CABLE,

JOHN R. BOGAN, Clerk.   PROPRIETOR.

3

2

4

5. In 1902 the Chippewa Hotel was built on the site of the old Wendell Custom House. It was managed for years by George and Susan Arnold.

6. While most guests enjoyed their stay at the John Jacob Astor House, Richard Hulbert, a local merchant who took his meals there, did have a complaint as told in his diary in 1890.

7. Business was good at the Astor House on this day when the guests assembled to be photographed. Most of the people on the front porch are band members.

McLEOD HOUSE,
MACKINAC, MICH.

This House is now open for the reception of guests. It has been repaired and enlarged, and furnished with entire new furniture. Its proximity to the Steamboat Landings, Places of Amusement, and business part of the town, makes it desirable for the Business Man and Pleasure-seeker, while the Invalid can rest under the **Extensive Piazzas**, and view the entire Town, Harbor, Fort, and Islands of the Straits, etc.

☞ An obliging Porter will be in attendance at the Boats to take charge of Baggage and conduct Passengers to the House.

R. McLEOD, Proprietor.

MACKINAC, *June* 18, 1862.

5

Mackinac, Mich. Dec. 9th 1890
Miss Effie Cable, daughter of James F. Cable, Landlord, and owner of the John Jacob Astor House, asked me while Shopping in my Store yesterday, the following question — If you were taken Sick, in your Store, would you come to the Astor House to stay, or would you, remain in your Store — I made her no reply — A few days since, I was attacked by a severe Bowel Complaint, which I believe was the result of some food, eaten at the Table, of the (John Jacob Astor House,) probably Boiled Oat Meal — I cured myself by using Dr. H. Kermotts Extract of Black Berry — Richard. P. Hulbert

Library of Congress 6

7

1. By 1887 Mackinac Island was one of the country's most famous summer resorts. Steamboat travel to northern Michigan was supplemented by several railroads that had pushed their tracks to the Straits. Although ordinarily fierce competitors for the tourist trade, three of these transportation companies, the Michigan Central and the Grand Rapids and Indiana railroads, and the Detroit and Cleveland Navigation Company joined hands to form the Mackinac Island Hotel Company. The result was the construction of one of the largest summer hotels in the world. Originally called "Plank's Grand Hotel" after its first operator, John Oliver Plank, an experienced manager from New England, it soon became known simply as Grand Hotel.

2. The Grand Hotel was a spectacular hotel in an impressive setting. Built high on a bluff overlooking the Straits of Mackinac, its huge size made it clearly visible from both Mackinaw City and St. Ignace. Its pleasing Grecian architecture was a sharp contrast from the usual gingerbread Victorian buildings. Clear white pine, Michigan's finest, was used throughout. Its 627-foot porch was the longest of any summer hotel in the world. When this photograph was taken in 1891 the building was about half its present size. The building in the center was the dining hall which was separated from the hotel to lessen the danger of fire, but joined by a long covered passageway.

3. Constructing the hotel was a mammoth job. Dozens of carpenters worked during the spring and summer of 1887. The St. Ignace *News* reported that in April, with the snow hardly off the ground, over thirty teams and wagons were being used to haul building materials from the downtown dock. The figures were not at all impressive to these village cows that took a morning swim beside the government pasture. When this land was leased to the hotel for a golf course, the road separating the pasture from the hotel property and its adjoining fence ceased to exist.

4. The Grand Hotel's opening in 1887 attracted wealthy and distinguished people from major midwest centers. From Michigan came such lumber barons as the Algers, Newberrys and Blodgetts. Adolphus Busch, the brewer from St. Louis, brought his family. Chicago was well represented by the Potter Palmers, Marshall Fields and the meat packers, Armours and Swifts. Later there were many ordinary mortals like these folk who assembled on the longest porch in 1910 to hear some selections by the hotel orchestra.

One 1895 visitor described his impressions: "Upon entering the hotel we went to the parlors, which were on the main floor at one side of the large rotunda office. Near them were the reading, writing and smoking rooms and some parlor bedrooms for invalids. At the other side of the office was the dining-room. It occupied at least one third of the length and the entire breadth of the building and was two stories high. It could evidently accommodate many hundreds of guests at one seating.

"At the upper end was a balcony for the orchestra, of which the Grand is so proud. For my own part, the music was not needed to aid in disposing of the tempting viands which were regularly set before us, but it certainly added vastly to my enjoyment of the meal hours.

"We found the guest rooms large, airy and elegantly furnished. The elevator and call bells placed us in easy reach of the office and the electric lights and gas were quite metropolitan. The rooms were offered us at $3 to $5 per day and we chose those of medium price, making special terms, of course, on account of our long stay."

5. The artist took a little liberty with this 1900 drawing. It was big, but not that big! Henry Weaver from the Planters Hotel in St. Louis operated the Grand for a few years early in the century. Despite the fact it was the most expensive place to stay on the Island, the short summer season and the enormous staff required to run the hotel made it unprofitable. Happily it has survived the usual fate of most 19th century resort hotels.

2

The Grand Hotel

ACCOMMODATIONS
FOR 1000 GUESTS

STRICTLY FIRST-CLASS   MACKINAC ISLAND
MICHIGAN

THIS FAMOUS
RESORT HOTEL

OPENS FOR THE SEASON JULY FIRST AND CONTINUES
UNTIL LATE IN SEPTEMBER

FOR RATES ADDRESS
HENRY WEAVER
PLANTERS HOTEL
ST. LOUIS, MO.

THE PLANTERS
ST. LOUIS
RATES, $2.00 TO $4.00

2

1

1. So the Victorian visitors had a wide choice of hotels at rates ranging from $1 a day at the Lozon to $5 at the Grand. And like all tourists everywhere, they soon set out to see the sights. These ladies are standing at Point Lookout above Sugar Loaf.

2. The best way to get around was by carriage, and, as you can see, there was no shortage of carriages-for-hire on Main Street in 1905. In fact, it was sometimes hard to avoid the hackman's persistent shouts that only *he* knew the Island and could give you the most informative ride.

At times Main Street was a veritable wall of hacks as their drivers waited patiently for the next lake boat arrival. Until the early 1940's the drivers operated independently and scaled their fees according to how many of the Island's attractions they covered.

3. Very important visitors usually chose the more impressive Victoria carriages like these on Market Street in 1884.

4. Then it was possible to get away from the crowd by renting a nice little private buggy — just you and your lady and a horse who would not hold his head and right front leg still for the photographer

3

4

Clarke Historical Library

5

6

5. But if you wanted a crowd, there was nothing better than the small, cozy brake that gave an opportunity to show off your finery. The dress styles of the 1890's featured ruffles, flounces, bustles, petticoats, bonnets and parasols for every occasion. The social ritual of elegant resorts included clothes for a morning promenade and changes for luncheon, afternoon tea and evening receptions. It was true, as Mark Twain put it, "Clothes make the man; naked people have little or no influence on society." The lady holding the white parasol is Mrs. Potter Palmer of Chicago, who was a frequent summer visitor to Mackinac Island.

6. The best place to get a bird's eye view of the Island was at Fort Holmes. There was little left of the fortification the British had built in 1812 after their capture of the Island. Some say the blockhouse had been blown apart by American artillery practice after the Americans regained possession of Fort Mackinac in 1815, and the wood was used to build the stable in the gardens below the fort. At any rate an 1886 National Park superintendent built a 20-foot platform on the highest point of the Island to replace an earlier one built in 1856. From here the panorama was spectacular. Not only could you see Fort Mackinac, the village, docks and mainland, but some of the extraordinary limestone formations for which the Island is famous.

1

2

guard house, or prison, where discipline was administered. Wi
overnment stables, blacksmith shop, granary, company's garde
A chapel is also provided. Were every other vestige of civilization
sland, the garrison of Fort Mackinac would go on the even te
rithout the slightest inconvenience.

The ancient features of the fort proved fully as interesting as
epresented, and the discipline and appearance of the troops real
nartial enthusiasm. The morning evolutions are not to be com
to the dress parade, w
on pleasant afternoons
and which every visitor

The view out to se
ments is truly magnifice

Striking out directl
the fort, through the
upon two curious relics

One was a quarry
which had evidently
industry in its day.

Near it wa
ruin, an old lim
date. The ne
wild and unta
hard to pictur
of busy indust

3

4

1. One of the most unusual was Sugar Loaf, a great limestone rock or, as geologists call it, a stack which rose abruptly some 75 feet from level ground.

Sugar Loaf was the result of water action thousands of years ago on the softer limestone, leaving the hard breccia masses intact, though pocked with numerous caves and indentations. For the Indians Sugar Loaf had a special significance as the home of the Great Spirit, Manibozho. They said it was so named because it was once a bee hive and every crack was filled with honey.

2. Along the shore road in 1905 a Victorian sightseer points out an unusual mainland feature. It was a man's world, and scholars of the 19th century believe women found an escape from male domination and an emotional outlet in travel. Many women painted and wrote of their experiences, real or imagined. They were avid collectors and "botanized" with considerable relish. But they never, never pursued their interests dressed informally. High necked blouses, long skirts and enormous hats were always visible, and for what was not visible, they took Constance Larymore's advice in 1902, "Always wear corsets even for tete a tete home dinners or warmest evenings. There is something about their absence almost as demoralizing as hair in curling pins."

3. On this page from an 1895 guidebook published by the Detroit and Cleveland Steam Navigation Company, a well bustled young lady is shown poking around the famous "Crack-in-the-Island." Indian legend held that the crack is haunted by a giant demon who attempted to descend to the depths of the Spirits of the Dead but was repulsed and now clings desperately to the edge of the fissure. If you step on his fingers, sickness, loss of wealth and misfortune in love are some of the calamities that could befall you.

4. On the east end of the Island was Arch Rock. Here, too, the forces of nature had fun, and the result was a 50-foot bridge of rock rising abruptly 146 feet above the lake.

5. Arch Rock was not only a great place to see, it was also a place to have your picture taken. What could be more daring than to go out on the arch itself and defy the vertical drop as these 1888 tourists did.

6. Visitors seemed to vie with each other in studied casualness as they posed for this photograph in 1895.

7. A favorite picnic spot was Devil's Kitchen along the beach. Years of wind and water erosion had left shallow caverns which were good places to make a fire with the unlimited supply of driftwood.

7

5

6

1

2

1. Bicycling was both fun and practical. Cedar-lined trails and roads connected the downtown hotels with all the natural and historical "curiosities" of Mackinac Island. These 1895 cyclists have stopped near Robinson's Folly.

2. Boating was fun, too. Several rental places along the harbor had canoes, row boats, and Mackinac craft available for those who would venture out in the Straits.

3. The three-sail Mackinac boat, which was the 19th century workhorse of the fur trader and fisherman, was easily handled by the novice sailor.

4. Uninhabited Round Island offered a chance to get away from the crowd. Note the bag of groceries (Or is it litter?) in the foreground.

5. Not everyone was adventurous enough to row to neighboring Round Island. But if you did, the view of Mackinac Island was worth the effort. Grand Hotel is in the center of the picture while part of Fort Mackinac is at the extreme right.

6. Where there's water, there's likely to be fish. This successful expedition in 1900 returned to the Island with a nice lake trout (left) and a mess of yellow perch.

3

4

5

1

Mackinac Island Historical Society

2

3

4

6

7

Library of Congress

1. Was there ever a tourist who did not relish a shopping expedition? A gift for the folks back home, a "bargain" picked up from a local merchant who underestimated its value, a piece of native handicraft, or simply a souvenir that would be a tangible reminder of a summer vacation — Well, the Mackinac Island visitor had a wide choice of shops happy to oblige. In this 1875 view of the business district looking west, the building on the left is Wendell's Custom House, but they sold snowshoes, Indian-made baskets, mococks of maple sugar and, as the sign states, "Stereoptic View of the Great Arch and Sugar Loaf. Books." For years the store was operated by Theodore Wendell, who traded merchandise with the Indians for their products.

2. Throughout the late 19th century and well into the 20th, Indians from neighboring areas found Mackinac a good market during the summer season. These squaws have set up their teepee of mats alongside one of the docks, where some interested tourists look on.

3. The earliest merchandisers on Mackinac Island were the Indians. This group is selling handicrafts in front of the soldiers' garden in 1905.

4. The "Indian curiosities" shown in this rare interior photograph of an 1890 shop included corn husk dolls, woven mats and baskets of all shapes and sizes. On the pole in the center are snowshoes and effigy pipes. Regional Indians had been supplying this kind of merchandise to the white visitors for generations.

5. Most of the Indian-made products were sold in the local souvenir shops. Because of its popularity with the visitors, many shop owners featured this type of merchandise until the supply was exhausted in the early years of the 20th century.

6. Looking east along Main Street in this 1900 view, the false-front shops on the left feature tourist gifts. The group of ladies look none too happy as they reach the end of the boardwalk and have to venture into a rather littered street. The building immediately behind them is the old Post Office, but by this date the postal service had moved across the street and down near Wendell's. The Mackinac House (center, dark columned) has been rebuilt after the fire of 1887. The farthest building on the left side of the street is Foley's art gallery and souvenir store. Note the little platform jutting from the center window.

7. The photographer who took this picture (Foley?) stood on that platform about 1905 to shoot this scene of a group of sailors marching past. Note the new post office on the left under the American flag. Fenton's Bazaar, one of the most patronized Island shops, is the tall, dark building on the extreme right. The dark-trimmed building with two chimneys at the center of the picture is the Palmer House.

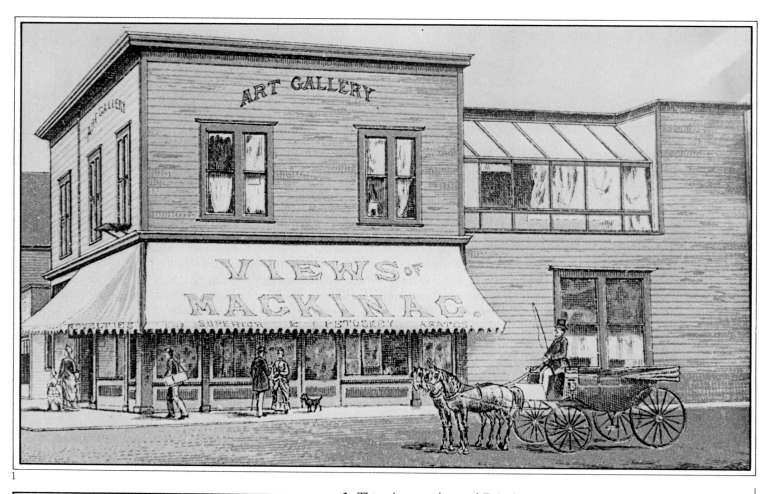

FENTON'S
INDIAN BAZAAR,

MACKINAC ISLAND, MICH.

The Largest and
Best Assortment in the
Northwest of
Rare Shells,
Minerals,
Lake Superior Agates
and Amethysts,
Views of Mackinac
National Park,
Feather Fans,
Moccasins,
Florida and Japanese
Goods,
And All Kinds of
CURIOSITIES.

A varied and beautiful
Line of
Moose Hair,
Porcupine-Quill,
and Sweet-Grass
WORK,
Including
Scented Table-Mats.
Canoes,
Satchels,
Portfolios,
Reticules,
Handkerchief Boxes,
Miniature Mococks
of Maple Sugar,
Florida Ornaments,
Grasses, Etc.

WHITMAN'S FAMOUS CONFECTIONS AND CHOCOLATES

IMPORTED AND DOMESTIC CIGARS.

FOR BEAUTY AND VARIETY OF GOODS,

C. B. Fenton's Indian Bazaar

CHALLENGES AND DEFIES COMPETITION.

1. This photo-etching of Foley's was made about the same time. But here the little platform is below the first window! Why? Note the window skylights on the right of the building. Before the age of flash bulbs, natural and exterior lighting had to be used for indoor portraits. Foley's burned to the ground in 1895.

2. The front of Charles Fenton's Indian Bazaar was indeed impressive. James Doud, an elderly resident in 1936, recalled the second floor was the Opera House, and he remembered seeing the McKeen and Campbell actors perform *East Lynne* in 1875. He also said that Fenton, who was a former Fort Mackinac officer, installed the first soda fountain in the downstairs store. It was a success all right, but the soda was so "fizzy you had to close your eyes to drink it." After the Opera House era, the second floor was used by William H. Gardiner, another popular Island photographer.

3. After 1880 Fenton's had a new neighbor on the left. This is Dr. Bailey's "National Park Drug Store." The general merchandise store was started by Levi Gray in 1854. His daughter, Sarah, married the Fort Mackinac doctor, who transformed the business to a drug store and gift shop.

4. Dr. John R. Bailey was a long-time resident of Mackinac Island. He served for many years as the only doctor and, after the Civil War became the garrison physician as a Brevet Lt. Colonel in the U. S. Volunteers. Interest in Mackinac history led him to publish a guidebook in 1895 which he called "Mackinac, formerly Michilimackinac." He also served on the Mackinac Island State Park Commission.

ESTABLISHED 1845.

JOHN R. BAILEY,

DEALER IN

DRUGS and MEDICINES

TOILET ARTICLES,

And all other Goods usually found in a First-Class Drug Store.

"ANNALS OF FORT MACKINAC,"

BOOKS, STATIONERY,

GUIDE-BOOKS, MAPS, CHARTS, ETC.

Pure Wines and Liquors for Medicinal Purposes.

PRESCRIPTIONS CAREFULLY COMPOUNDED.

DR. JOHN R. BAILEY,

U.S. Examining Surgeon,

(Late Surgeon U. S. Vols., late Attending-Surgeon at Fort Mackinac,)

RESIDENCE, adjoining ISLAND HOUSE.   OFFICE, IN DRUG STORE.

4

Scalps! Scalps!

Call and see the Indian DUDES and DUDINES; lineal descendants of HIAWATHA and MINNEHAHA.

Call and hear the BLOOD-CURDLING CHIPPEWA WAR-WHOOP; the DEFIANT OTTAWA BATTLE-CRY; the VICTORY-SHOUT of the IROQUOIS; the HEART-RENDING HURON DEATH-SONG; and get tickets for the DAKOTA SCALP-DANCE.

Indian Pipes, Wampum, War-Clubs, Tomahawks, Scalping Knives, Scalps, Bows and Arrows, Boomerangs, etc., etc.

Annals of Fort Mackinac.

Price, 25 Cents.   *By Mail, 30 Cents.*

S. HIGHSTONE
MACKINAC ISLAND.

1

Edward J. McAdam

TWO STORES ON WATER STREET AND A STAND IN THE GRAND HOTEL

INDIAN CURIOSITIES

and an assortment of Fancy and other Goods too numerous to mention

MOSS AGATES, FANCY JEWELRY AND SOUVENIRS

BOOKS, MAGAZINES, PAPERS AND FINE STATIONERY

Agent for Dr. John R. Bailey's "Great Book," "MACKINAC, formerly Michilimackinac;" it sells as our goods go, "like hot cakes."

FRUITS AND NUTS IN SEASON   MACKINAC ISLAND MICHIGAN

3

2

6

Mackinac Island Historical Society

1. Highstone's and McAdam's were two gift shops west of Bailey's Drug Store.

2. John W. Davis operated one of the most important general stores on Main Street. His father, John Davis, was a Frenchman who changed his name when he emigrated to America in the early 1800's. John W. came to Mackinac in 1866, bought a grocery business, and developed it into the Island's finest. The choice groceries, fruits, and vegetables were bought not only by Mackinac residents, but by cottagers on the mainland. In 1908 Davis built a larger store of brick, the only one on the street. He died in 1918 at the age of 93.

3. The likeness of Mr. and Mrs. John W. Davis is preserved in this pre-Civil War daguerreotype.

4. Another pioneer merchant was Richard P. Hulbert, who operated on the corner of Astor and Main Streets. Hulbert was born in Sheffield, England in 1820 but came to Erie, Pennsylvania at an early age. In 1851 he established a dry goods business on Mackinac Island and for the next forty years supplied "dress goods generally" to Islanders and summer visitors alike. The very patriotic Hulbert flew the American flag above his store on all special occasions.

5. Hulbert kept a diary from 1887 to 1891 in which he recorded every vessell that docked at the Island, as well as commentary and observations on the local scene. This is his entry for September 21, 1887.

6. One of the principal Island grocery stores and the only one surviving to this day was Doud's Mercantile Company. It was located at the head of the main dock, until that building burned in 1943. For over fifty years it was operated by James Doud, whose father, Stephen, like so many Irishmen, emigrated to America and Mackinac Island in the late 1840's.

7. There is absolutely no connection between Mackinac Island and the Oriental goods that began to be featured widely about 1910. But, like so many resort shops of a later day, "curiosities" that could not be readily bought at home were highly salable. Or, to put it another way, tourists will buy almost anything!

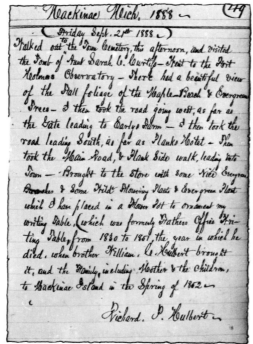

1. In this 1910 view of Main Street looking west, Persian rugs are advertised by a shop in the new Chippewa Hotel, as well as by the two stores on the right.

2. Shopping could make a man very thirsty. What better way to refresh himself than to step into this unidentified 1890 saloon. These cigar-smoking, properly attired young men may be off one of the many private yachts that made Mackinac Island a port of call. A City ordinance of 1887 stated, "All saloon bars or taverns where liquor is sold . . . shall be closed on the first day of each week, commonly called Sunday . . . . The word closed in this section shall be construed to apply to the back door as well as the front door." These gentlemen may just be enjoying a bottle of Budweiser, but there is no indication of their occupation. The army reported in the summer of 1887 that it was necessary to patrol the park with soldiers to break up confidence games and arrest "3 card monte men."

3. E. W. Puttkammer, who came to Mackinac Island in 1892 ("I learned to walk there.") recalls going to the "theatre" on the extreme left. Edison's Kinetoscope featured a 5 cent program of lantern slides to the accompaniment of a piano player. The Main Street also had an ample number of restaurants.

4. This restaurant was next to Wendell's on the water side of Main Street. Puttkammer recalls that it was operated by a Mrs. Ford of Grand Rapids, who served excellent meals. When the Chippewa Hotel was built in 1903, the building was razed.

5. Three of the Island's principal hotels appear in this scene photographed with a telephoto lens from the harbor in 1894. The Grand Hotel on the bluff is flanked by the Palmer House on Main Street and John Jacob Astor House back on Market Street. Coal has obviously replaced wood as the principal fuel. Hulbert's shop is the first building to the right of the dock.

6. Traveling was more fun if you could share your experiences with the less fortunate back home. The Victorian traveler used the time-honored post card to relate his adventures and impressions. Scenes of Fort Mackinac, Arch Rock, Sugar Loaf and the Grand Hotel were favorites. All the hotels had writing rooms where the lady or gentleman traveler could remind a friend that he was missed. For the non-creative writer, this card could be purchased in any of the gift shops on Main Street.

7. The United States Post Office on the west end of Main Street near the Palmer House was the place to get your mail and a good rundown on what was new or, at least, the latest rumors.

1

Library of Congress 2

3

4

5

Here I am at Mackinac Island
Enjoying its sights and cheer
Everything's great and I am feeling fine
But oh! How I wish you were here.

POST OFFICE

1

2

3

6

7

1. In the days before the Polaroid and Instamatic cameras, picture taking was the work of professionals. Many photographers, including William H. Gardiner, set up shop on Main Street. Gardiner's was located in the towered Fenton's Bazaar. He actually photographed his subjects in a small addition to the rear of the building. The glass panels were designed to get as much morning sun as possible.

2. Gardiner probably took this portrait of himself and friend Buster about 1910.

3. A Turkish potentate's boudoir? No, it's the sales room of Gardiner's Photographic Studio. Here you made arrangements to have your portrait done before some exotic painted backdrop, or perhaps in an outdoor Island setting with some of your friends. It was not easy to move all the camera and dark room paraphernalia out of the studio in these pioneering days of photography, but Gardiner was glad to oblige.

4. Oh, come now! That's not the way to ride a bicycle through that beautiful landscape.

5. About seventy years ago these young ladies and gentlemen walked up fort hill, found a nice grassy spot with an interesting background and held their breath for about fifteen seconds while Mr. Gardiner snapped their picture. It turned out very well.

Mackinac Island Historical Society

6. So well, in fact, that the photographer led another group to the same spot a little later. This is certainly as pretty a selection of young Victorian ladies as ever vacationed on Mackinac Island.

7. For the most spectacular view of the harbor and city of Mackinac Island, there was "inspiration point" at the southeast corner of Fort Mackinac. Here on the ramparts of the fort, where British and American cannon once guarded the Straits joining Lakes Huron and Michigan, these five couples stand at attention one summer day in 1899 to be preserved on film for posterity. We will probably never know who they are, why the lady on the left moved her head and what the gentleman is pointing at.

8. If these Gardiner pictures look posed, it is because they were. Film speed in the 1890's was slow by today's standards, so the subjects had to stand very still — sometimes up to a minute. To get a feeling of informality, the photographer placed them in what he felt was a natural position, doing natural things. But today their appearance seems as stiff as department store mannequins.

9. Another favorite location for picture taking was the long porch of the Grand Hotel. On this day nearly a hundred guests, whose badges indicate they were observing some special occasion, peer intently into Mr. Gardiner's lens. Is the matriarch in the center front an individualist, or did the photographer have her study her address (?) book for some sort of dramatic relief? Nobody said "cheese."

1

2

3

Katherine Bond

4

1. Gardiner was more interested in the summer visitors than in the people who served them, so pictures like this are very rare. These are waiters and porters, probably from one of the large excursion boats that came to the Island.

2. This well-staged before and after "party" was typical of early attempts at photographic humor. Perhaps the celebration with cigars and wine marks the end of another hectic tourist season.

3. In the 1870's and 80's changes in Mackinac's churches reflected the growing summer population. Ste. Ann's, which originally stood between Market and Main Streets at the west end of town was moved to the east end near Mission Church as the result of a gift of land from Madame La Framboise. Some of the bodies in the graveyard were moved to a new cemetery in the center of the Island on land furnished by the military. But a few graves remained, at least until 1888, as this picture indicates. Note the tombstone at the extreme right.

4. Hulbert walked along here in 1888 making his observations. Much later another old Mackinac resident, Miss Helen Donnelly, who owned Cloghaun, the building on the right, said that her brother, while plowing in the old cemetery, uncovered some foundations he thought were of the church.

5. Richard Hulbert recorded the names of those who remained in 1888. Here is a page from his diary.

The Old Mackinac Cemetery, on the Street in which the Astor House is built

The following persons, Still remain in this Old Cemetery

Many of them Ancient Burials — Some have been removed

(50)

September 1888

Sept. 22   City of Athena — Gazelle
(Sunday)
Algomah   (Sunday 23)

23   Visited the Old Town Cemetery, on the South West Corner of the Block, next to my Store — Most of the persons, or bodies, intered in this Cemetery have been removed to the New Cemeteries on the Hill, near Fort Mackinac — The following is a list of the Bodies still remaining in this Cemetery, Sept 23d 1888 — with the Inscriptions on the Stones —

In Memory (No-1)

Mrs. Abigail F. Read, Legate wife of Capt. Thomas. C. Legate U. S. Artillery, born in Boston Mass. June 28th 1789 —
Died at Mackinac Aug: 11th 1821

1

5

1

2

1. In 1832 under the direction of Father Mazzuchelli, the church was moved to this location near Mission Point. (a)

2. This new Ste. Ann's Roman Catholic Church dates from 1874, but the steeple was not completed until much later. Catholic activity in the Straits dates from 1670, when Father Claude Dablon established the first mission on the Island. The center of Jesuit teaching, however, was transferred to St. Ignace on the mainland the following year when Marquette built his mission. After 1715 and until 1780 the mission was based at Michilimackinac on the south side of the Straits. The parish records dating from the 1700's are still preserved in this Island church.

3. In 1882 Trinity Episcopal Church was built on Fort Street at the foot of Fort Mackinac. Legend has it that an officer pledged a sizeable donation to the building fund on the condition that the church be located conveniently to the garrison. The local congregation took him up on it, but before they could collect, he was transferred. By then the church was already constructed. Reverend John O'Brien, an Episcopal army chaplain, preached both to the soldiers and villagers in the mid-century. In the 1870's these Protestant services were held on the second floor of the soldiers' barracks.

4. Prior to the railroad that reached the Straits in 1881, everything was transported by boat. From January to April every year the Straits were frozen, and what mail, food and supplies came to Mackinac had to be transported over a dangerous ice bridge. It's no wonder Fort Mackinac fired a three-gun salute and the residents rang the Mission bell when the first vessel arrived that April 10, 1888. Hulbert duly noted the event.

5. The caption recorded on the picture tells the story.

6. These 1890 Mackinac Islanders are crossing the ice with a load of firewood which they have cut on Bois Blanc Island, about four miles away. The soldiers usually contracted with local men to supply wood for the garrison.

7. The winters were long and the snow was deep on Main Street when this photograph was taken in front of the Palmer House. The man in the white apron is the local butcher.

3

April 10th 1888

Hoisted my Colors the United States Flag on the Flag Staff on my Store while the Rail Road Steamer St Ignace was breaking her way to St Ignace on the North Side of Bois Blanc Island — She arrived at the outer edge of the Ice three miles East of Bois Blanc Island about day light to day the 10th of April — She received a Salute of Three Guns from Fort Mackinac — The Mison Church Bell was rung when she passed through the Harbor of Mackinac —

4

Mike Lennon's Last Trip
On the Old Mackinaw Route
with Soo Mail.
Winter of 1886-'87.

5

Mackinac Island Historical Society

6

Clarke Historical Library

7

Mackinac Island Historical Society

THE PARK

With Mackinac Island firmly committed to tourism, some important governmental policies brought about significant physical changes. In 1875 the Congress of the United States established the second National Park on the Island. While this action preserved the natural beauty of the Island, the leasing of land along the bluffs resulted in private construction of large summer homes. The National Park stimulated other private building, most notably in Gurdon S. Hubbard's Annex. These cottages not only introduced new architectural features to Mackinac, but their owners' need for services greatly affected the Island's permanent residents.

The idea of preserving parts of Mackinac Island for the enjoyment of the people was enlarged with the transfer of jurisdiction from Federal to State hands in 1895. Fort Mackinac had outlived its usefulness, and its garrison had moved to other military reservations. The State of Michigan agreed to take over the land, as well as Fort Mackinac, and to maintain the whole as a permanent State Park.

The Mackinac Island State Park Commission took important steps to fulfill this trust and to promote the concept of a park for the use of summer visitors. The soldiers' garden was transformed into a small formal park that soon became one of the Island's most popular areas. The old government pasture was leased to the Grand Hotel for a public golf links. In 1923 the Commission doubled the total park area by purchasing the old Early farm, including the site of the 1814 battlefield. Other property of historical significance later acquired included the Edward Biddle House, Astor Company retail store, Indian Dormitory, Mission Church, and Island House hotel, so that now approximately 82 per cent of Mackinac Island is under the protection of the State of Michigan.

1. In 1873 steps were taken in Congress to preserve Federal lands on Mackinac Island for posterity, when Michigan's Senator Thomas W. Ferry (who was born in the Mission school his parents operated) introduced a resolution withdrawing from settlement all of the Federal land on Mackinac Island excepting Fort Mackinac and setting it aside for the "health, comfort and pleasure, for the benefit and enjoyment of the people." Congress acted that year to establish Yellowstone in the Territory of Wyoming as the first National Park, and in 1875 the second park was created on Mackinac Island in accordance with Ferry's resolution. It included about half the Island.

Sincerely Yours,
T. W. Ferry.

1

MAP OF
MACKINAC ISLAND,
MICHIGAN.

Entered according to Act of Congress in 1882, by
D. H. KELTON.

REGULATIONS FOR THE DISTRIBUTION AND ACCOUNTABILITY OF THE PROCEEDS OF
LEASES AND OTHER REVENUES IN CONNECTION WITH THE
NATIONAL PUBLIC PARK AT MACKI-
NAC, MICHIGAN.

THAT PORTION OF THE ISLAND OF MACKINAC, IN THE STRAITS OF MACKI-
NAC, WITHIN THE STATE OF MICHIGAN, SET APART BY THE ACT OF CONGRESS AP-
PROVED MARCH 3, 1875, AS A NATIONAL PUBLIC PARK, AND PLACED UNDER THE EX-
CLUSIVE CONTROL OF THE SECRETARY OF WAR, WILL BE PUT IN CHARGE OF AN OF-
FICER OF THE ARMY DETAILED FOR THAT PURPOSE BY THE SECRETARY.

SUCH OFFICER SHALL EXECUTE, ON BEHALF OF THE UNITED STATES, SUBJECT
TO THE APPROVAL OF THE SECRETARY OF WAR, LEASES FOR BUILDING PURPOSES OF
SMALL PARCELS OF GROUND IN SAID PARK, AS PROVIDED FOR BY THE AFORESAID
ACT. HE SHALL RECEIVE THE MONEY PAYABLE ON ACCOUNT OF SAID LEASES, AND,
UNDER THE DIRECTION OF THE SECRETARY OF WAR, DISBURSE THE SAME, AS WELL AS
ALL OTHER REVENUES WHICH MAY BE SET APART OR COME INTO HIS POSSESSION FOR
THE PURPOSE, FOR THE IMPROVEMENT OF THE SAID PARK, IN THE MANAGEMENT OF
THE SAME, AND IN THE CONSTRUCTION OF ROADS AND BRIDLE-PATHS THEREIN.

THE LEASES ABOVE REFERRED TO, SHALL BE MADE IN ACCORDANCE WITH THE
PRESCRIBED FORM MARKED NATIONAL PUBLIC PARK, FORM NO. 1, AND WHEN MADE
SHALL BE DISPOSED OF AS IS PRESCRIBED BY ARMY REGULATIONS FOR LEASES
MADE BY OFFICERS OF THE QUARTERMASTER'S DEPARTMENT.

THE OFFICER SHALL AVAIL HIMSELF OF THE DEPOSITORIES DESIGNATED BY
THE TREASURY DEPARTMENT FOR THE SAFE-KEEPING OF THE PUBLIC FUNDS COM-
ING INTO HIS POSSESSION FOR PURPOSES CONNECTED WITH THE PARK; SHALL DE-
POSIT SUCH FUNDS IN SAID DEPOSITORIES AND DRAW THE SAME THEREFROM BY
CHECKS THEREON, SIGNING SAID CHECKS IN HIS OFFICIAL CAPACITY AND AS IN
CHARGE OF NATIONAL PUBLIC PARK; AND SAID OFFICER SHALL OTHERWISE BE GOV-
ERNED IN THE DISBURSEMENTS OF SUCH FUNDS IN THE MANNER PRESCRIBED BY
ARMY REGULATIONS GOVERNING DISBURSING OFFICERS OF THE ARMY, SO FAR AS
THE SAME SHALL BE APPLICABLE.

ALL ACCOUNTS FOR PURCHASES AND OTHER EXPENDITURES SHALL SET FORTH
A SUFFICIENT EXPLANATION OF THE OBJECT, NECESSITY AND PROPRIETY OF THE
EXPENDITURE.

SUCH ACCOUNTS SHALL BE MADE OUT ON FORMS TO CORRESPOND WITH THOSE
OF THE QUARTERMASTER'S DEPARTMENT, AND THE OFFICER SHALL MAKE REPORTS
OF PERSONS AND ARTICLES HIRED, RETURNS OF PUBLIC PROPERTY, AND ACCOUNTS
FOR MONEYS RECEIVED AND EXPENDED UPON SIMILAR FORMS, AND SUCH ACCOUNTS
AND RETURNS, SUPPORTED BY PROPER VOUCHERS, SHALL BE RENDERED TO THE QUAR-
TERMASTER GENERAL IN THE MANNER PRESCRIBED BY ARMY REGULATIONS FOR MON-
EY AND PROPERTY ACCOUNTABILITY OF OFFICERS OF THE QUARTERMASTER'S DE-
PARTMENT.

THE QUARTERMASTER GENERAL SHALL CAUSE A RIGID ADMINISTRATIVE SCRU-
TINY TO BE MADE IN HIS OFFICE OF SUCH ACCOUNTS AND RETURNS, AFTER WHICH
THEY SHALL BE TRANSMITTED TO THE PROPER OFFICERS OF THE TREASURY DE-
PARTMENT FOR SETTLEMENT

THE REGULATIONS + + + ARE APPROVED.

THE FORM OF LEASE + + + IS APPROVED AS THE FORM OF LEASE TO BE
USED IN CONNECTION WITH THE MACKINAC NATIONAL PARK.

THE COMMANDING OFFICER OF THE POST (FORT MACKINAC), FOR THE TIME
BEING, IS HEREBY DESIGNATED AS THE AGENT OF THE SECRETARY OF WAR TO MAKE
LEASES AND PERFORM OTHER DUTIES IN CONNECTION WITH THE MACKINAC NATION-
AL PARK REQUIRED TO BE PERFORMED BY THE SECRETARY OF WAR. HE WILL RE-
PORT ANNUALLY, AND AS MUCH OFTENER AS MAY BE NECESSARY, TO THE SECRETARY
OF WAR, THROUGH THE QUARTERMASTER GENERAL OF THE ARMY, IN RELATION TO THE
DUTIES HEREBY IMPOSED UPON HIM.

ROBERT T. LINCOLN,
SECRETARY OF WAR.

WAR DEPARTMENT, DECEMBER 27, 1884.

2

Chicago, August 8. 1849

Major Charles H. Larnard, U.S.A.
Commanding at Fort Mackinac

Dear Sir

Residing as
I do in the City of Chicago, I am desirous of securing
a comfortable arrangement for spending the hotter portion
of the summer months at Mackinac.

The accommodations for receiving visitors at Mackinac
are so meagre that families are frequently unable on their
arrival to obtain quarters at all convenient or comfortable.

The Government as you are aware retain as a
Military Reservation the larger portion of the Island, and
include in such reserve, the entire bluff on the front and
East side of it, comprising all the most desirable situations
for building upon in that vicinity.

I beg leave therefore, through you and with your
approbation, to make application to the Quarter Master
General for permission to erect a summer Lodge upon the
Bluff East of the Garrison.

This point is selected because of its easy access - its
airy and sightly position - its convenience to the Hotel
under the bluff, to which it can be readily connected by a
flight of stairs - and, because of its not appearing to be
wanted for any purpose in connection with the post
as a Military station.

On the third page you will find a diagram

of the premises which I desire permission to occupy during
the pleasure of the Government - It lies in a triangular
form, is bounded on the west by the enclosure East of
the Garrison, on the south by the Bluff and the rear
of the village lots and the Indian Agency lot under the
Bluff, and North Easterly by the road leading from the Fort
to the Mission House, extending Easterly, to the junction of
said Road, with the bluff, and containing about three
acres.

This ground has never been occupied or improved
in any way, and has nothing upon it of value, to be
removed or destroyed - It is at present in a very rough
state and the improvements I propose to make upon
it would add to its sightliness & increase its value.

Should permission be granted me to occupy and build
upon the premises here described, I stand ready to obligate
myself in any proper way to remove from and re-deliver
peaceable possession of the same at any time when required.

Should you concur with me in the opinion that
the Government would not be subjected to any inconvenience
or embarrassment in granting any request for the occupancy
of the premises referred to, during and subject to its pleasure,
you will oblige me by presenting my application to the
Quarter Master General with such comments as you may
think it proper and your duty to make.

With great respect
I remain
Your Obt. Servt.
W.B. Ogden

2. The National Park was placed under the control of the Secretary of War and administered through the commanding officer at Fort Mackinac. Although the lands were "withdrawn from settlement" in 1875, the fort officer was allowed to lease "small parcels of ground" for building purposes and to use the proceeds from these rentals for improvement of the park. This Federal policy (which also applied to other National Parks) established an important precedent which was continued by the State when it acquired the park in 1895.

3. The leasing of park land grew out of a long history of requests from Island visitors who wished to establish summer homes where they could escape the heat and hay fever of southern areas. This letter written to the military by a Chicago resident is, no doubt, typical of many received from summer visitors. What is surprising is the early date of 1849.

4. The most desirable areas on which to build summer homes in the National Park were on the east and west bluffs. In 1883 the bluffs were platted into lots of about 100-foot frontage. Those east of the fort were the first to be leased, and by 1886 the commanding officer reported that three summer homes had been built on the east bluff and one on the west. This 1895 photograph shows the east bluff on the extreme right. Note the barren appearance of the hill.

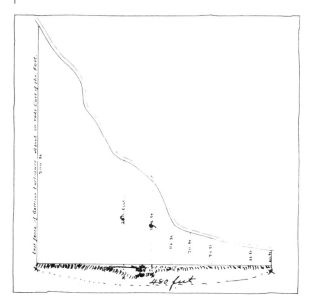

3

4

1

ALFRED G. COUCHOIS,

PRACTICAL

Carpenter,

Joiner, and

Painter,

MACKINAC ISLAND, MICH.

Mr. Couchois offers his services to those
who contemplate building Summer Residences on the Island of Mackinac.

REFERENCES:

The Citizens of Mackinac Island generally and all Officers
of the U.S. Army, who have been stationed at Fort
Mackinac, during the past ten years.

4

5

6

2

7

3

1. *The American Heritage Dictionary* says that a cottage is a small summer house used for vacation. Granted that the word "small" is relative, the cottages on the bluffs seem to stretch it a bit. Most contained from ten to twenty rooms with large and spacious wrap-around porches. Many had distinctive conical appendages that were reminiscent of medieval castles. This cottage of Henry Duffield of Detroit on the east bluff overlooking the harbor was one of the first to be built in 1885.

2. The cottages were built by wealthy midwesterners who came each July with their families, servants, pets and steamer trunks to relax in their favorite watering place. These west bluff houses facing the mainland were built in the mid-1890's by (left to right): Alexander D. Hannah, David Hogg, and John Cudahy of Chicago, and Mrs. Susan Blodgett Lowe, the daughter of a prominent Grand Rapids lumberman.

Mrs. Robert Doud

8

3. By 1900 most of the available land along the east bluff had been leased and cottages built. The Federal government was achieving its objective of attracting tenants who would build, and through their lease payments, help pay for the operation of the park. However, the cost of maintenance of these houses and the right of the local city government to tax them as personal property made the cottages an increasingly heavy financial burden on their owners. During the depression of the 1930's many of the homes were given up.

4. Many of the cottages were constructed by local carpenters who were skilled craftsmen, having learned their trade in the Island cooper shops during the commercial fishing era.

5. One of the most prominent carpenters was Patrick Doud, who was 86 when this picture was taken in 1947. His father came to the Island with the wave of Irish immigrants in the 1840's and 50's and established a barrel-making business. Doud built many of the houses along the bluffs and in the annex.

6. Doud's own house (right) on the west lake shore was typical of Island homes at the turn of the century.

7. One of Pat Doud's first big jobs was a cottage he built on the east bluff for Milton Tootle of St. Joseph, Missouri. He recalled that in the interior he used Georgia yellow pine "for the beauty of its grain," while the exterior was of Michigan's finest wood, the white pine. Tootle, who was fond of gardening, had a celebrated Japanese garden in his back yard. One of the large trees he pruned to resemble a sailboat. A businessman who wanted to be an architect, he designed part of the interior of the cottage himself. He was particularly fond of his magnificent staircase.

8. Pat Doud built the Charles Truscott home on Market Street in 1900. This is one of the very few pictures in existence showing a house under construction. Doud is second from the right.

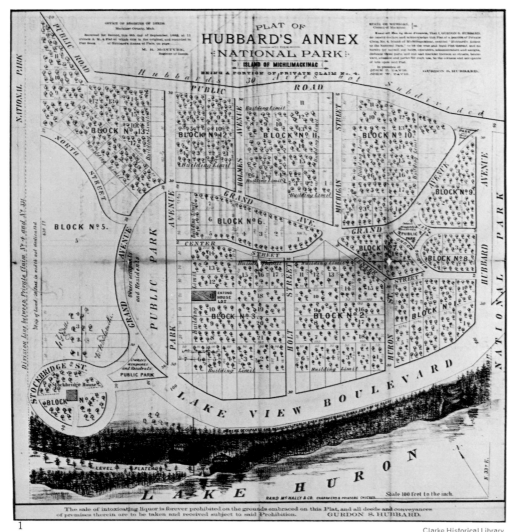

PLAT OF
HUBBARD'S ANNEX
TO THE
NATIONAL PARK
ISLAND OF MICHILIMACKINAC
BEING A PORTION OF PRIVATE CLAIM N° 4.

Scale 100 feet to the inch.

The sale of intoxicating liquor is forever prohibited on the grounds embraced on this Plat, and all deeds and conveyances of premises therein are to be taken and received subject to said Prohibition. GURDON S. HUBBARD.

Clarke Historical Library

Building Lots

ON THE

Island of Mackinac, Mich.

FOR SALE.

THOSE who intend to build Summer Residences on Mackinac Island, will find the most desirable Lots, at very reasonable prices, on the western part of the Island, around the rock known as "Lover's Leap" and above the caves known as the "Devil's Kitchen."

An 80-acre lot has been neatly laid out and until the Colony, already started, is as large as is desired, lots will be sold on very advantageous terms to the purchaser.

The view from this bluff is the finest on the Island, overlooking the entrance to Lake Michigan with its numerous Islands and Light-Houses, and in full view of St.Ignace and Mackinaw City.

For Particulars, address

GURDON S. HUBBARD,

243 Locust Street, CHICAGO.

1. The principal summer home subdivision on private land was developed by Chicagoan Gurdon S. Hubbard in the early 1880's. His Annex to the National Park was laid out with ample lots, wide boulevards, a public park, even an "eating house" lot (left center). But teetotaler Hubbard forever prohibited the sale of intoxicating liquor in this development.

2. The "Annex" attracted prominent residents from many midwestern cities. E. W. Puttkammer of Chicago, whose father was one who built his own cottage, recalled that most of the others had been built by one of two contractors who made them all alike! However, the houses were extensively altered throughout the years. In the early 1890's drinking water was carted by barrel from the spring near the fort. Rain water was used for washing. In 1895 one cottager installed a small pump which pumped water from the lake near Devil's Kitchen through a small iron pipe and, Mr. Puttkammer added, constantly broke down, to everyone's consternation. This gingerbread-decorated Annex cottage was typical of many built in the late 1890's.

3. Of all the things Victorian cottages had in common, the most obvious were the porches. As in the interiors, there was no shortage of furnishings. Here a gentleman is reading the late news while he relaxes amid floral splendor: The hanging basket of natural flowers and vines, a large urn of freshly cut daisies, and, above his head, a small Indian-made birch bark canoe featuring a potted plant. If this was not enough, there is another plant on the table and a large floral wall hanging to the right of the cut glass window.

4. Enclosed porches were also very colorful. Wicker furniture was decorated with floral-patterned cushions, and Japanese motifs, such as the lanterns shown here, were popular. The dozens of small window panes were picturesque and designed for the time when domestic help was readily available.

5. The bedrooms in the 1890 summer homes were both decorative and practical. Wood was the principal building material, and it was used throughout the house. Wainscotting, walls and ceilings of wood were invariably found in the bedrooms. Here a gentleman's room featured the usual couches with their loosely stuffed pillows. Kerosene lamps, Persian throw rugs and a painted brass spindled bed with a rather lumpy mattress were perhaps not the same quality as in his home in Chicago, but, after all, this was a "cottage," and one could expect to rough it a bit.

3

4

1. The Victorian lady's bedroom was somewhat more elaborate. A better grade of wood wainscotting with an interesting variation in design gives this room much character. The feminine touch is obvious in the lace doilies on the dresser and the canopied dressing table. The small writing desk in the far corner was a staple piece of furniture in all bedrooms. There is a considerable amount of restraint in the use of wall features in this bedroom. Notice the crucifix above the bed, and the candle on the small bedside table. Hanging from the wall lamp over the dresser at left are a couple of small Indian-made wicker baskets — probably as good a use as there is for this souvenir.

2. Empty wall space or, for that matter, empty table space was to be avoided at all costs. This study and living room, which could be separated by the hanging drapes, is typically late 19th century. The walls again are variations of wainscotting, varnished to retain the natural look as well as to show off the Georgia pine grain. Another advantage of wood walls was that it was easy to hang pictures. Riding scenes and horses were favored by this owner. The desk is cluttered with mementos.

3. There was very little paint in evidence in the interiors. Wicker furniture, which was so widely used, was left in a natural state. Walls and floors were only varnished, and this created a dark and mysterious atmosphere that the Victorians seemed to like. It also accounts for the large number of ceiling and wall light fixtures, as well as the white lace curtains. In this living room, a pair of binoculars used to watch a passing boat rests on the table. The piano stool on the right serves a more exotic purpose than was intended.

4. Pat Doud said that there lived on Mackinac Island a Frenchman identified only as "La Duke," a master carpenter who did most of the railings and spindles for the Mackinac cottages. This beautiful open stairway is, no doubt, an example of his work. The pride of local craftsmanship and the extraordinary carpentry skill is evident everywhere in these Island homes. Many of their present owners have retained the unusual period furnishings.

5. If there was not room on the porch, or if you just wanted to get away for a little privacy, there was always the back yard. This east bluff yard had a tree seat and a group of rustic chairs amid a multitude of flowering plants. There is just enough of a vista cut through the trees to see neighboring Round Island and the passing boats.

6. Some of the formal flower gardens with dozens of blooming shrubs set off by terraced stone retaining walls show the influence of Japanese landscaping. The stone is native limestone, and it is laid exactly as Governor Sinclair's masons would have done in the 1780's.

7. Stonecliffe, one of the most spectacular summer homes, was built by Michael Cudahy, one of the three "meat packing" brothers who owned cottages on the Island at one time or another. Built on the northwest side in what was known as Benham's Annex, it not only commanded a magnificent view of the Straits of Mackinac but set a standard of opulence unequaled in the Island's history.

1

2

4

5

6

7

1

1. The new fangled automobile may be coming to the streets back home, but on Mackinac Island the horse is still king. And if your father owned a summer home here, he could afford to buy you a nice pony like this one.

2. Hay rides were popular, and you could have a lot of fun even if the ride was chaperoned by such a forbidding figure as appears on the right. This bunting-decorated farm wagon and the American flags mean a 4th of July outing.

3. Meanwhile, back at the cottage there is another party in full swing. Note the huge Japanese lantern in the center of the picture. To the right of the stairway on the porch is a wicker lawn chair. This interesting piece of furniture was designed to protect Victorian ladies from the undesired sun, as "getting a tan" was definitely not the objective of a summer vacation. But such an all-protective device had a great disadvantage: You could only see in one direction. To remedy this, manufacturers began to install small portholes on either side.

4. In the late 1890's the game of golf became an important recreational activity. The Grand Hotel built its course in 1904, but as early as 1899 the cottagers leased some land in the center of the Island for a club and golf links which they called Wawashkamo. The course was laid out over the old 1814 battlefield site. According to tradition, Major Andrew Holmes fell not far from this clubhouse.

5. During the 1880's many permanent residents bought property in Private Claim No. 110 near the center of the Island and built their homes there. The settlement has come to be known as Harrisonville, so named after President Benjamin Harrison. This view is looking south. At upper right is Round Island, now part of the Hiawatha National Forest, and beyond is the Island of Bois Blanc.

2

4

Mackinac Island Historical Society

3

5

1

History Division, Michigan Department of Sta

1. Toward the end of the 19th century the pattern of tourism changed. Large excursion boats and the railroads brought more visitors, but they stayed a shorter time. Even if your schedule allowed only a few hours to browse through the shops or sit with the children on the grass in Marquette Park, it was a vacation to remember.

2. In 1894 the War Department withdrew the Army garrison from Fort Mackinac. Although the soldiers had previously been absent from Mackinac for short periods, now the decision was made to abandon the post permanently. Because its commanding officer was also the superintendent of the National Park, this duty would have to be undertaken by another governmental agency. In 1895 the United States offered to transfer the park and the fort to the State of Michigan, subject only to the condition that it be used "as a state park and for no other purpose" and that, if it should cease to be so used, "it shall revert to the United States." Michigan accepted the proposal, and the Legislature created a Park Commission of five members to "lay out, control and manage the park" and to employ a superintendent. It was the first park in the state and, like the National Park, a prime tourist attraction.

3. The Act creating the Mackinac Island State Park Commission referred to a "park fund" and limited the "debts and obligations" to the "funds at hand." This was significant because it meant the Commissioners were expected to raise at least part of the cost of maintaining the facility in the same way the Federal government had done, namely, leasing land for private purposes compatible with park use. Consequently, at its first meeting held in the Grand Hotel in 1895 the Commission raised the yearly land lease rental for summer cottages from $25 to $100. It also gave consideration to requests to lease land below the fort in the old fort gardens.

4. In 1898 the Park Commission issued three leases on land to the right of the old gardens. They specified the cottages should be erected within one year and cost at least $3,000. The building in the foreground on the right was owned by George T. Arnold, who operated the local ferry company and later built the Chippewa Hotel. Mrs. S. A. Hert of Jeffersonville, Indiana built her cottage next door.

5. In 1901 the Commission issued a fourth lease to Lawrence A. Young of Chicago for land west of the fort and one of the most spectacular views on the Island, even though immediately below was the village pasture. This beautiful summer home was designed by Frederick W. Perkins, a prominent Chicago architect, and built by Patrick Doud. The carpenter had a crew of 75 Island men working on this cottage. Unfortunately, the job cost more than his contract price, but he recalled 46 years later that Mrs. Young had been so delighted with the house that she handed him a check for $500 more than the agreed figure.

3

Burton Historical Collection

4

5

1. One of the most significant early decisions of the Commission was to deny a request to lease the fort gardens for the construction of a hotel. Instead, it set aside the grounds below Fort Mackinac to be used "for an ornamental and recreational park" to be known as "Pere Marquette Place." In 1906 after some delay the "potato patch," as it was sometimes called, was transformed by formal plantings and wide gravel walkways. On the lower left is the base for the Marquette memorial.

2. It must have been a proud day for Dr. John Bailey, who stands before the statue the day before the formal dedication.

3. The memorial statue was primarily the idea of Peter White of Marquette, Michigan, an original member of the Commission and pioneer lumber and mining figure. The $2,000 cost of the statue was paid through public subscription and the donation of White himself. Many state school children contributed. On September 1, 1909 the park and statue were dedicated. When the American flags gently parted, the huge crowd saw the bronze figure of Father Jacques Marquette, S. J., one of the earliest missionaries in the Straits, who with Louis Joliet discovered the Mississippi River in 1675.

1
Library of Congress

2
Robert Bailey
3

4. The speeches of the day were delivered from the porch of the soldiers' barracks at Fort Mackinac. U. S. Supreme Court Justice William R. Day, who had a summer home in the Annex, delivered the principal address. It was his hope that the thousands who come from "towered cities and the busy marts of trade to find health and recreation on the Island shall learn as they look upon this statue new lessons of duty, of self reliance and that faith in high ideas which characterized every act of Jacques Marquette from early manhood to the grave."

5. It was a nice day, incidentally. Those umbrellas are to keep off a warm afternoon sun.

6. Had Marquette been able to return for the ceremonies he might have been surprised at the portly bearded figure representing him for he was only 39 years old when he died. But the sculptor depicted the symbolism of this remarkable missionary who gave his life in the cause of exploration and Christianity.

Mackinac Island Historical Society

1

2

Robert Bailey

1. Everyone knows that automobiles are prohibited on Mackinac Island, but what is not generally known is that the request to use these vehicles came very early in the history of the auto. In 1901 John Cudahy asked the Commission whether he could bring over his machine. At that time there were probably less than a couple hundred of these vehicles in Michigan and certainly few suitable roads. The Commission, no doubt, did considerable soul searching before turning him down to protect the "safety of visitors within the park." To this day, or perhaps I should say especially in this day, few have doubted the wisdom of that courageous decision.

2. Steps were taken to control the use of carriages-for-hire in the park. Although the licensing of this sort of commercial operation on public property seems a natural thing today, in 1901, when the state authorities established a fee of $1 to $3 for the horse-drawn rigs, the local city government and the owners fought it bitterly. Eventually a landmark decision of the State Supreme Court in 1902 (Kerrigan v. Poole) established that the right to require a license to use park roads was within the authority of the Mackinac Island State Park Commission because these roads were not city streets but were driveways established by the Federal government, and in 1895 their control and use was transferred to the State of Michigan. In this picture Patrick Kerrigan, the plaintiff, stands next to his carriage and boarding house.

3. The National Park and military reservation included about 1,100 acres or about 50 per cent of the entire area of the Island. Since 1895 the Commission has acquired over 600 additional acres. The largest piece, purchased in 1925, included most of Private Claim No. 1, the old Dousman and Early farm. This put the site of the 1814 American-British battle under State protection. The important site was officially recognized by the Michigan Historical Commission, and a State plaque now marks the battlefield.

4. A great many physical changes took place on Mackinac Island in the past 150 years, yet the surprising fact is that so much remains the same. The small boats from the mainland still enter the harbor and discharge their cargoes and passengers on docks that were there in 1820. The business district is still bracketed between a curving main thoroughfare that follows the water and an arrow-straight Market Street. The eastern section of town from the Indian Dormitory to Robinson's Folly is considerably more built up, particularly near the Mission buildings, but beyond the line of 80-year old east bluff cottages, the land would not seem strange to the prehistoric Indians. While some of the fort buildings were constructed late in the military occupation, as we have seen, the walls, sally ports, officers' stone quarters and blockhouses remain as Sinclair and his immediate American successors built them.

5. Market Street still means business on Mackinac Island although the only furs are on the shoulders of some of its visitors. The business of the Island is History. It is the most important product, and the whole economy of the Island is geared to the summer visitation of a half million tourists. The Edward Biddle house and the old Astor retail store where Dr. Beaumont treated St. Martin are museums, as is the Robert Stuart house shown here. The Island community and the State of Michigan recognize the economic as well as the aesthetic value in their preservation of these historic structures.

BATTLEFIELD OF 1814

Here in this area on Aug. 4, 1814, an American force battled the British in a vain attempt to recapture the island which the British had seized at the outbreak of the War of 1812. Coming ashore at what is known as British Landing, the Americans under Col. George Croghan soon ran into strong resistance as they advanced inland. An attempt to outflank the British line was repulsed by Indians hidden in thick woods and resulted in the death of Maj. Andrew Holmes. Croghan withdrew when he found that he could not defeat the British.

MICHIGAN HISTORICAL COMMISSION REGISTERED SITE NO. 188

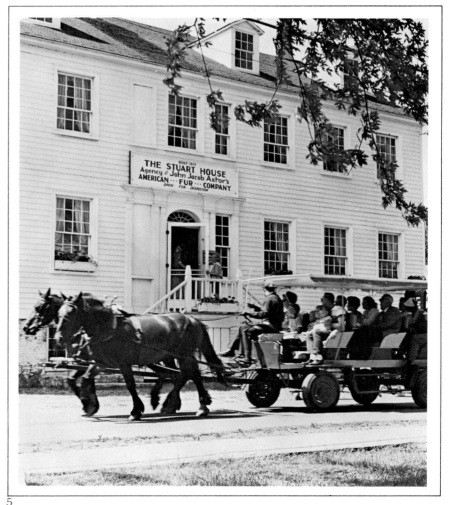

3   5

1. Has Mackinac changed since 1780? Physically there have been changes, of course, as in any community. Perhaps nowhere has the change in the village now City of Mackinac Island, been more apparent than from the ramparts of Fort Mackinac at a spot called inspiration point. This series of pictures taken from that vantage point shows some remarkable changes in architecture.

a

d

e

h

i

History Division, Michigan Department of State

c

g

k

1

1. The changes in the remarkable natural limestone formations are not perceptible, but that is hardly surprising when we realize that nature took thousands of years in creating them. The caves, Arch Rock, Robinson's Folly, Lover's Leap, Crack-in-the-Island and Sugar Loaf have been photographed and described thousands of times. In an age when man has been to the moon and done about everything else, these examples of natural formations are still amazing for him to see.

2. Bicycling is the best way to see the Island, as it has been since the turn of the century. It has been over 160 years since the British landed here, but, other than a couple of picnic tables, a bench and an official Michigan Historical Commission marker, the invaders would find little else unfamiliar. Just as William Gardiner did nearly a century ago, a photographer has pointed his camera in the direction of two very pretty girls.

3. Although most summer tourists spend less than a day on Mackinac Island, many come for longer visits. The Island hotels still try to provide the elegant service that began during the Victorian era. None is doing a better job than Grand Hotel, which has succeeded in blending a 19th century atmosphere with modern comforts and conveniences. Its guests no longer move in with steamer trunks and nursemaids for an extended summer sojourn. More likely they are salesmen for an insurance company who found it impossible to attend this convention alone when their wives learned it was to be held on Mackinac. Like many before them, they find it hard to believe that the porch is over twice the length of a football field.

4. The summer cottages have changed very little. That is rather surprising when one considers that they were built in a day when domestic help was easy to employ. Despite tremendous upkeep costs

2

3

and the difficulties of getting away for an extended vacation, most of Mackinac's homes have survived. The Young cottage was purchased by the State of Michigan in 1945 to be a summer residence for the Governor. Today the view from his front porch is of the Grand Hotel golf course with a lonely player, which Mr. Young would probably agree is better than the old government pasture.

5. The art of shopping still thrives on Main Street. Indian-made corn husk dolls and baskets are no longer featured, and you cannot buy an oriental rug anymore, but some of the shops have unusual souvenirs that will help recollect a visit to Mackinac. Many of the old gift shops now compete in selling the "best" fudge. The morning carriage line-up is not much different, although the rubber-tired, wide-seated buggies are designed for efficiency and comfort. The horse is still the means of transport on Mackinac Island.

6. In this view of Main Street looking west, there is much that is familiar. On the right side, Alford's Drug Store is on the site of the old wine and liquor store. The old Fenton's Bazaar/Opera House is next door. Now, however, the distinctive tower has been removed for safety reasons. Some of the photographs in this album were made from glass negatives that were discovered in Gardiner's Studio on the second floor. The small building beyond, once Bailey's Drug Store, is now a book store. Further on is the familiar Murray Hotel, no longer the "New Murray." The trees are in the small city park where the "New Mackinac House" once stood. The dark building further down the street (left center) is the John W. Davis building, the only brick structure on the street.

7. It all started in 1780 during the American Revolution when Governor Patrick Sinclair decided to move the fort to Mackinac Island.

5

6

4

7

Eugene T. Petersen, Superintendent, Mackinac Island State Park Commission, has directed the reconstruction of historic Fort Michilimackinac at Mackinaw City and the restoration and historical interpretation work at Mackinac Island since the outset of this program in 1958. A former United States Marine communications officer and a graduate of Marquette University (B.S., 1942 and M.A., 1947) and the University of Michigan (Ph.D., 1952), he has taught European, American, and Michigan history at the University of Detroit and the University of Michigan. He was director of the State Historical Museum in Lansing for several years before going to Mackinac.

INDEX